*A dream is real so long as it . . . . we awake,
we do not pass from unreality to reality; we pass
from a lower state of reality to a higher one. Is it
not possible that there is a state of awareness higher
still, compared with which the limited satisfactions
of everyday life are no more lasting than a dream?*

EKNATH EASWARAN

COMPANION VOLUME

❧

PASSAGE MEDITATION

Bringing the Deep Wisdom of the Heart

into Daily Life

Timeless Wisdom

Passages for Meditation from
the World's Saints & Sages

EKNATH EASWARAN

NILGIRI PRESS

First edition. First printing May 2008

ISBN 978-1-58638-027-4

Library of Congress Control Number 2008921640

Printed on 100% post-consumer recycled paper

Publishers Cataloging-in-Publication block will be

found on the last leaf of this book.

This book is a compact edition of a fuller anthology,
God Makes the Rivers to Flow, *with a new preface
and additional passages.*

Eknath Easwaran founded the Blue Mountain Center of
Meditation in Berkeley, California, in 1961. The Center is a
nonprofit organization chartered with carrying on Easwaran's
legacy and work. Nilgiri Press, a department of the Center,
publishes books on how to lead a spiritual life in the home and
community. The Center also teaches Easwaran's eight-point
program of passage meditation at retreats worldwide.

For information please visit www.easwaran.org,
call us at 800 475 2369 (USA) or 707 878 2369
(international and local), or write to us at
The Blue Mountain Center of Meditation,
Box 256, Tomales, CA 94971–0256, USA.

Table of Contents

In the Company of Saints & Sages

THIS BOOK IS a collection of passages with the power to transform lives, drawn from the world's great spiritual traditions. It is a companion to my book *Passage Meditation*, which describes a program for putting that power to work – for bringing the deep wisdom of the heart into daily living.

I was in the midst of a very busy career in the English department of a university in India when I began to develop this program in my own life. That story is told in *Passage Meditation;* here I would like simply to add a few words about what the richness of this discovery meant to me – and why meditating on passages like these makes this method of meditation so effective and so universal.

In Kerala state, South India, where I grew up, the new year is ushered in with a ceremony many centuries old. The night before, while most of the family is asleep, a special shrine is assembled with all kinds of lustrous objects – yellow flowers, brassware, gold jewelry, ripe fruits, lighted oil lamps – arranged around a mirror draped with garlands. The next morning, each member of the family is led to the shrine with eyes closed and asked, "Would you like to see the Lord?" We open our eyes, and shining in the midst of this bright setting we see our own face in the glass. It is a beautiful reminder of the divinity in each of us – the viewer and everyone else around.

Naturally, the reminder tends to get forgotten later, as life closes in again. But in my home, whenever one of us children began to misbehave, my grandmother had only to ask, "Do you remember where you saw the Lord on New Year's?"

The passages in this book are like that New Year mirror. They show us our original goodness. They remind us that whatever mistakes we may have made in the past, however self-centered our words or behavior might be today, at the center of our personality lies a spark of the divine that can never be extinguished, does not even have to be earned, for it is an essential part of our nature as human beings.

When you and I look into a mirror, we see a familiar face with a distressing tendency to show fatigue or age. But that is not what the mystics see. They look at us – through us, into us – and see something transcendent, luminous, timeless, "the Face behind all faces":

I look into the mirror and see my own beauty;
I see the truth of the universe revealing itself as me.
I rise in the sky as the morning sun, do not be surprised . . .
I am Light itself, reflected in the heart of everyone.

— FAKHRUDDIN ARAQI

> Every particle of the world is a mirror.
> In each atom lies the blazing light
>   of a thousand suns.

— MAHMUD SHABESTARI

> Radiant is the world soul,
> Full of splendor and beauty,
> Full of life . . .

— ABRAHAM ISAAC KOOK

Words like these are not just poetry. They are a passionate attempt to describe the direct, personal encounter with a reality beyond words, put into words by men and women overwhelmed by the desire to share that experience with anyone who will listen. When we hear with open hearts, the words stir a response within us. We glimpse in them a reflection of our own true Self. The wonderful potential latent in us begins to shine, as a possibility we can not only imagine but long for and begin to live by.

This is the real purpose of this book: to provide not just a collection of inspiring poetry, but a mirror for helping us translate the lofty vision of the world's great spiritual traditions into our daily lives.

How this can be done is the subject of my introduction, but I can give a simple illustration. Imagine beginning each day absorbed in meditation on passages like this from Francis of Assisi:

Lord, make me an instrument of thy peace.

Where there is hatred, let me sow love;

Where there is injury, pardon;

Where there is doubt, faith;

Where there is despair, hope;

Where there is darkness, light;

Where there is sadness, joy.

Or this, from the Buddha:

Just as a mother with her own life

protects her child, her only child, from harm,

so within yourself let grow

A boundless love for all creatures. . . .

Strive for this with a one-pointed mind;

your life will bring heaven to earth.

When you step out into the workaday world enveloped in words like these, the words go with you. Gradually they become part of you, assimilated into your character and consciousness. They provide armor to protect you from the stress and hurry of the day – the armor of patience, compassion, wisdom, courage, love.

More than that, they become your friends. When you get caught up in the heat of the moment, the words come to you and tug at the sleeve of your mind. "An instrument of peace, remember? As a mother protects her only child?" For if this original goodness is in each of us – you and me – then it is within everyone else as well. Surprisingly, perhaps, the only way we can reveal the divinity in ourselves is to focus on it in those around us.

These words ring with power – and not simply the power of words. Words go no deeper than experience. If a neighbor says, "Go sell what you have and give it to the poor," will we take it seriously? Yet the same words from Jesus have been changing lives for thousands of years. A nobleman in third-century Egypt, a would-be troubadour in Assisi, an obscure nun teaching school in Calcutta hears them and puts them into action, transforming not just one life but countless thousands. Words from this depth of the heart never lose their power.

And don't they speak with one voice, these lovers of God? Which is the Catholic nun, which the Sufi poet, which the Indian sage? Like heights above the timberline, where no tree can grow, on these heights of the spirit no distinctions can arise. However varied the paths, when we actually make this journey, we cannot help but end up at the same place.

I'm often reminded of nineteenth-century explorers' search for the highest mountain in the world. Tibetans pointed to Chomolungma, Nepalis to Sagarmatha, Chinese to Shengmu Feng. In Darjeeling, Westerners looking for "Peak XV" were directed to Deodungha. All, of course, turned out to be talking about the same peak, best known today as Mt. Everest.

Similarly, though the men and women in this book naturally fall back on the language of their own times and traditions, they are not repeating dogma or theory. They are telling us what they have *seen*, describing a place they have actually gone to and discovered to be their home – and then come back to tell us, over and over, that this is our home as well.

I like to think of this place as a country, a vast realm in the depths of consciousness beyond the frontier of personal separateness – a land of unity where all of creation is one. Others prefer terms that are cozier and more personal, scaled to human dimensions. For Teresa of Avila it is an "interior castle"; for Augustine, a city; in the Upanishads, "a secret dwelling in the lotus of the heart." Whatever the language, however, all the world's great mystics agree with one voice that this place at the center of the soul is where we really belong. "God is at home," insists Augustine; "we are abroad." Until we discover this for ourselves, we remain exiles, wanderers, tourists with a growing sense of being strangers in a strange land. Our main job in life is to find this place in the heart where we belong; then we are at home wherever we go:

> After much wandering I am come home,
> Where turns not the wheel of time and change....
> Listen to Ravidas, just a cobbler:
> All who live here are my true friends.

After decades of meditation, I can say the same of the saints and sages you will meet in this book. All are my true friends – constant companions whose words remind me daily of the divinity latent in us all. I hope they will become your friends as well.

❧

The Lord is in me, the Lord is in you,
As life is in every seed.
O servant! Put false pride away
And seek for him within you.

KABIR

Introduction

IN ANCIENT INDIA lived a sculptor renowned for his life-sized statues of elephants. With trunks curled high, tusks thrust forward, thick legs trampling the earth, these carved beasts seemed to trumpet to the sky. One day, a king came to see these magnificent works and to commission statuary for his palace. Struck with wonder, he asked the sculptor, "What is the secret of your artistry?"

The sculptor quietly took his measure of the monarch and replied, "Great king, when, with the aid of many men, I quarry a gigantic piece of granite from the banks of the river, I have it set here in my courtyard. For a long time I do nothing but observe this block of stone and study it from every angle. I focus all my concentration on this task and won't allow anything or anybody to disturb me. At first, I see nothing but a huge and shapeless rock sitting there, meaningless, indifferent to my purposes, utterly out of place. It seems faintly resentful at having been dragged from its cool place by the rushing waters. Then, slowly, very slowly, I begin to notice something in the substance of the rock. I feel a presentiment . . . an outline, scarcely discernible, shows itself to me, though others, I suspect, would perceive nothing. I watch with an open eye and a joyous, eager heart. The outline grows stronger. Oh, yes, I can see it! An elephant is stirring in there!

"Only then do I start to work. For days flowing into weeks, I use my chisel and mallet, always clinging to my sense of that outline, which grows ever stronger. How the big fellow strains! How he yearns to be out! How he wants to live! It seems so clear now, for I know the one thing I must do: with an utter singleness of purpose, I must chip away every last bit of stone that is not elephant. What then remains will be, must be, elephant."

When I was young, my grandmother, my spiritual guide, would often tell just such a story, not only to entertain but to convey the essential truths of living. Perhaps I had asked her, as revered teachers in every religion have been asked, "What happens in the spiritual life? What are we supposed to do?"

Granny wasn't a theologian, so she answered these questions simply with a story like that of the elephant sculptor. She was showing that we do not need to bring our real self, our higher self, into existence. It is already there. It has always been there, yearning to be out. An incomparable spark of divinity is to be found in the heart of each human being, waiting to radiate love and wisdom everywhere, because that is its nature. Amazing! This you that sometimes feels inadequate, sometimes becomes afraid or angry or depressed, that searches on and on for fulfillment, contains within itself the very fulfillment it seeks, and to a supreme degree.

Indeed, the tranquility and happiness we also feel are actually reflections of that inner reality of which we know so little. No matter what mistakes we may have made – and who hasn't made them? – this true self is ever pure and unsullied. No matter what trouble we have caused ourselves and those around us, this true self is ceaselessly loving. No matter how time passes from us and, with it, the body in which we dwell, this true self is beyond change, eternal.

Once we have become attentive to the presence of this true self, then all we really need do is resolutely chip away whatever is not divine in ourselves. I am not saying this is easy or quick. Quite the contrary; it can't be done in a week or by the weak. But the task is clearly laid out before us. By removing that which is petty and self-seeking, we bring forth all that is glorious and mindful of the whole. In this there is no loss, only gain. The chips pried away are of no consequence when compared to the magnificence of what will emerge. Can you imagine a sculptor scurrying to pick up the slivers that fall from his chisel, hoarding them, treasuring them, ignoring the statue altogether? Just so, when we get even a glimpse of the splendor of our inner being, our beloved preoccupations, predilections, and peccadillos will lose their glamour and seem utterly drab.

What remains when all that is not divine drops away is summed up in the short Sanskrit word *aroga*. The prefix *a* signifies "not a trace of"; *roga* means "illness" or "incapacity." Actually, the word loses some of its thrust in translation. In the original it connotes perfect well-being, not mere freedom from sickness. Often, you know, we say, "I'm well," when all we mean is that we haven't taken to our bed with a bottle of cough syrup, a vaporizer, and a pitcher of fruit juice – we're getting about, more or less. But perhaps we have been so far from optimum functioning for so long that we don't realize what splendid health we are capable of. This *aroga* of the spiritual life entails the complete removal of every obstacle to impeccable health, giving us a strong and energetic body, a clear mind, positive emotions, and a heart radiant with love. When we have such soundness, we are always secure, always considerate, good to be around. Our relationships flourish, and we become a boon to the earth, not a burden on it.

Every time I reflect on this, I am filled with wonder. Voices can be heard crying out that human nature is debased, that everything is meaningless, that there is nothing we can do, but the mystics of every religion testify otherwise. They assure us that in every country, under adverse circumstances and favorable, ordinary people like you and me have taken on the immense challenge of the spiritual life and made this supreme discovery. They have found out who awaits them within the body, within the mind, within the human spirit. Consider the case of Francis Bernardone, who lived in Italy in the thirteenth century. I'm focusing on him because we know that, at the beginning, he was quite an ordinary young man. By day this son of a rich cloth merchant, a bit of a popinjay, lived the life of the privileged, with its games, its position, its pleasures. By night, feeling all the vigor of youth, he strolled the streets of Assisi with his lute, crooning love ballads beneath candlelit balconies. Life was sweet, if shallow. But then the same force, the same dazzling inner light, that cast Saul of Tarsus to the earth and made him cry out, "Not I! Not I! But Christ liveth in me!" – just such a force plunges our troubadour deep within, wrenching loose all his old ways. He hears the irresistible voice of his God calling to him through a crucifix, "Francis, Francis, rebuild my church." And this meant not only the Chapel of San Damiano that lay in ruins nearby, not only the whole of the Church, but that which was closest of all – the man himself.

This tremendous turnabout in consciousness is compressed into the Prayer of Saint Francis. Whenever we repeat it, we are immersing ourselves in the spiritual wisdom of a holy lifetime. Here is the opening:

> Lord, make me an instrument of thy peace.
> Where there is hatred, let me sow love.

These lines are so deep that no one will ever fathom them. Profound, bottomless, they express the infinity of the Self. As you grow spiritually, they will mean more and more to you, without end.

But a very practical question arises here. Even if we recognize their great depth, we all know how terribly difficult it is to practice them in the constant give-and-take of life. For more than twenty years I have heard people, young and old, say that they respond to such magnificent words – that is just how they would like to be – but they don't know how to do it; it seems so far beyond their reach. In the presence of such spiritual wisdom, we feel so frail, so driven by personal concerns that we think we can never, never become like Saint Francis of Assisi.

I say to them, "There is a way." I tell them that we can change all that is selfish in us into selfless, all that is impure in us into pure, all that is unsightly into beauty. Happily, whatever our tradition, we are inheritors of straightforward spiritual practices whose power can be proved by anyone. These practices vary a bit from culture to culture, as you would expect, but essentially they are the same. Such practices are our sculptor's tools for carving away what is not-us so the real us can emerge.

Meditation is supreme among all these tested means for personal change. Nothing is so direct, so potent, so sure for releasing the divinity within us. Meditation enables us to see the lineaments of our true self and to chip away the stubbornly selfish tendencies that keep it locked within, quite, quite forgotten.

In meditation, the inspirational passage is the chisel, our concentration is the hammer, and our resolute will delivers the blows. And how the pieces fly! A very small, fine chisel edge, as you know, can wedge away huge chunks of stone. As with the other basic human tools – the lever, the pulley – we gain tremendous advantages of force. When we use our will to drive the thin edge of the passage deep into consciousness, we get the purchase to pry loose tenacious habits and negative attitudes. The passage, whether it is from the Bhagavad Gita or *The Imitation of Christ* or the Dhammapada of the Buddha, has been tempered in the flames of mystical experience, and its bite will . . . well, try it and find out for yourself just what it can do. In the end, only such personal experience persuades.

Now if we could hold an interview with a negative tendency, say, Resentment, it might say, "I don't worry! I've been safely settled in this fellow's mind for years. He takes good care of me – feeds me, dwells on me, brings me out and parades me around! All I have to do is roar and stir things up from time to time. Yes, I'm getting huge and feeling grand. And I'm proud to tell you there are even a few little rancors and vituperations running around now, spawned by yours truly!" So he may think. But I assure you that when you meditate on the glorious words of Saint Francis, you are prying him loose. You are saying in a way that goes beyond vows and good intentions that resentment is no part of you. You no longer acknowledge its right to exist. Thus, we bring ever more perceptibly into view our divine self. We use something genuine to drive out impostors that have roamed about largely through our neglect and helplessness.

To meditate and live the spiritual life we needn't drop everything and undertake an ascent of the Himalayas or Mount Athos or Cold Mountain. There are some who like to imagine themselves as pilgrims moving among the deer on high forest paths, simply clad, sipping only at pure headwaters, breathing only ethereal mountain air. Now it may sound unglamorous, but you can actually do better right where you are. Your situation may lack the grandeur of those austere and solitary peaks, but it could be a very fertile valley yielding marvelous fruit. We need people if we are to grow, and all our problems with them, properly seen, are opportunities for growth. Can you practice patience with a deer? Can you learn to forgive a redwood? But trying to live in harmony with those around you right now will bring out enormous inner toughness. Your powerful elephant will stir and come to life.

The old dispute about the relative virtues of the active way and the contemplative way is a spurious one. We require both. They are phases of a single rhythm like the pulsing of the heart, the indrawing and letting go of breath, the ebb and flow of the tides. So we go deep, deep inwards in meditation to consolidate our vital energy, and then, with greater love and wisdom, we come out into the family, the community, the world. Without action we lack opportunities for changing our old ways, and we increase our self-will rather than lessen it; without contemplation, we lack the strength to change and are blown about by our conditioning. When we meditate every day and also do our best in every situation, we walk both worthy roads, the *via contemplativa* and the *via activa*.

The passages in this book are meant for meditation. So used, they can lead us deep into our minds where the transformation of all that is selfish in us must take place. Simply reading them may console us, it may inspire us, but it cannot bring about fundamental, lasting change; meditation alone does that. Only meditation, so far as I know, can release the inner resources locked within us, and put before us problems worthy of those resources. Only meditation gives such a vital edge to life. This is maturity. This is coming into our own, as our concerns deepen and broaden, dwarfing the personal satisfactions – and worries – that once meant so much to us.

If you want to know how to use inspirational passages in meditation, you'll find full instructions on the Web at www.easwaran.org/learn or in the companion volume for this book,

Passage Meditation. The basic technique, duration and pace, posture, and place are all taken up, as part of a complete eight-point program for spiritual living – the program I have followed in my own life. Everything is covered there; here I would simply like to add a bit about the criteria I use in selecting passages like these for meditation.

We wouldn't use a dull chisel or one meant for wood on a piece of stone, and we should use suitable passages for meditation. We're not after intellectual knowledge, which helps us understand and manipulate the external world. We seek spiritual wisdom, which leads to inner awareness. There, the separate strands of the external world – the people, the beasts and birds and fish, the trees and grasses, the moving waters and still, the earth itself – are brought into one great interconnected chord of life, and we find the will to live in accordance with that awareness. We find the will to live in perpetual love. I think you'll agree there are very few books which can ever lead us to that.

The test of suitable meditation passages is simply this: Does the passage bear the imprint of deep, personal spiritual experience? Is it the statement of one who went beyond the narrow confines of past conditioning into the unfathomable recesses of the mind, there to begin the great work of transformation? This is the unmistakable stamp of authenticity. Only such precious writings can speak directly to our heart and soul. Their very words are invested with validity; we feel we are in the presence of the genuine.

The scriptures of the world's religions certainly meet this test, and so do the statements of passionate lovers of God like Saint Teresa, Kabir, Sri Ramakrishna, Ansari of Herat. And whatever lacks this validation by personal experience, however poetic or imaginative, however speculative or novel, is not suited for use in meditation.

But there is another thing to be considered: Is the passage positive, inspirational, life-affirming? We should avoid passages from whatever source that are negative, that stress our foolish errors rather than our enduring strength and wisdom, or that deprecate life in the world, which is precisely where we must do our living. Instead, let us choose passages that hold steadily before us a radiant image of the true Self we are striving to realize.

For the great principle upon which meditation rests is that we become what we meditate on. Actually, even in everyday life, we are shaped by what gains our attention and occupies our thoughts. If we spend time studying the market, checking the money rates, evaluating our portfolios, we are going to become money-people. Anyone looking sensitively into our eyes will see two big dollar signs, and we'll look out at the world through them, too. Attention can be caught in so many things: food, books, collections, travel, television. The Buddha put it succinctly: "All that we are is the result of what we have thought."

If this is true of daily life, it is even more so in meditation, which is concentration itself. In the hours spent in meditation, we are removing many years of the "what we have thought." At that time, we need the most powerful tools we can find for accomplishing the task. That is why, in selecting passages, I have aimed for the highest the human being is capable of, the most noble and elevating truths that have ever been expressed on this planet. Our petty selfishness, our vain illusions, simply must and will give way under the power of these universal principles of life, as sand castles erode before the surge of the sea.

Specifically, what happens in meditation is that we slow down the furious, fragmented activity of the mind and lead it to a measured, sustained focus on what we want to become. Under the impact of a rapidly-moving, conditioned mind, we lose our sense of freely choosing. But, as the mind slows down, we begin to gain control of it in daily life. Many habitual responses in what we eat, see, and do, and in the ways we relate to people, come under our inspection and governance. We realize that we have choices. This is profoundly liberating and takes away every trace of boredom and depression.

The passages in this collection have been drawn from many traditions, and you'll find considerable variety among them. Some are in verse, some in prose; some are from the East, some from the West; some are ancient, some quite recent; some stress love, some insight, some good works. So there are differences, yes, in tone, theme, cultural milieu, but they all have this in common: they will work.

As your meditation progresses, I encourage you to build a varied repertory of passages to guard against overfamiliarity, where the repetition can become somewhat mechanical. In this way, you can match a passage to your particular need at the time – the inspiration, the reminder, the reassurance most meaningful to you.

Nearly everyone has had some longing to be an artist and can feel some affinity with Granny's elephant sculptor. Most of us probably spent some time at painting, writing, dancing, or music-making. Whether it has fallen away, or we still keep our hand in, we remember our touches with the great world of art, a world of beauty and harmony, of similitudes and stark contrasts, of repetition and variation, of compelling rhythms like those of the cosmos itself. We know, too, that while we can all appreciate art, only a few can create masterworks or perform them as virtuosi.

Now I wish to invite you to undertake the greatest art work of all, an undertaking which is for everyone, forever, never to be put aside, even for a single day. I speak of the purpose of life, the thing without which every other goal or achievement will lose its meaning and turn to ashes. I invite you to step back and look with your artist's eye at your own life. Consider it amorphous material, not yet deliberately crafted. Reflect upon what it is, and what it could be. Imagine how you will feel, and what those around you will lose, if it does not become what it could be. Observe that you have been given two marvelous instruments of love and service: the external instrument, this intricate network of systems that is the body; the internal, this subtle and versatile mind. Ponder the deeds they have given rise to, and the deeds they can give rise to.

And set to work. Sit for meditation, and sit again. Every day without fail, sick or well, tired or energetic, alone or with others, at home or away from home, sit for meditation, as great artists throw themselves into their creations. As you sit, you will have in hand the supreme hammer and chisel; use it to hew away all unwanted effects of your heredity, conditioning, environment, and latencies. Bring forth the noble work of art within you! My earnest wish is that one day you shall see, in all its purity, the effulgent spiritual being you really are.

The Prayer of Saint Francis

Lord, make me an instrument of thy peace.
Where there is hatred, let me sow love;
Where there is injury, pardon;
Where there is doubt, faith;
Where there is despair, hope;
Where there is darkness, light;
Where there is sadness, joy.

O divine Master, grant that I may not so much seek
To be consoled as to console,
To be understood as to understand,
To be loved as to love;
For it is in giving that we receive;
It is in pardoning that we are pardoned;
It is in dying to self that we are born to eternal life. ✦

The Inner Ruler

The Lord is enshrined in the hearts of all.
The Lord is the supreme reality.
Rejoice in him through renunciation.
Covet nothing. All belongs to the Lord.
Thus working may you live a hundred years.
Thus alone can you work in full freedom.

Those who deny the Self are born again
Blind to the Self, enveloped in darkness,
Utterly devoid of love for the Lord.

The Self is one. Ever still, the Self is
Swifter than thought, swifter than the senses.
Though motionless, he outruns all pursuit.
Without the Self, never could life exist.

The Self seems to move, but is ever still.
He seems far away, but is ever near.
He is within all, and he transcends all.

Those who see all creatures in themselves
And themselves in all creatures know no fear.
Those who see all creatures in themselves
And themselves in all creatures know no grief.

How can the multiplicity of life
Delude the one who sees its unity?

The Self is everywhere. Bright is the Self,
Indivisible, untouched by sin, wise,
Immanent and transcendent. He it is
Who holds the cosmos together.

In dark night live those
For whom the world without alone is real;
In night darker still, for whom the world within
Alone is real. The first leads to a life
Of action, the second of meditation.
But those who combine action with meditation
Go across the sea of death through action
And enter into immortality
Through the practice of meditation.
So have we heard from the wise.

In dark night live those for whom the Lord
Is transcendent only; in night darker still,
For whom he is immanent only.
But those for whom he is transcendent
And immanent cross the sea of death
With the immanent and enter into
Immortality with the transcendent.
So have we heard from the wise.
    The face of truth is hidden by your orb

Of gold, O sun. May you remove the orb
So that I, who adore the true, may see
The glory of truth. O nourishing sun,
Solitary traveler, controller,
Source of life for all creatures, spread your light,
And subdue your dazzling splendor
So that I may see your blessed Self.
Even that very Self am I!

May my life merge in the Immortal
When my body is reduced to ashes!
O mind, meditate on the eternal
Brahman. Remember the deeds of the past.
Remember, O mind, remember.

O God of fire, lead us by the good path
To eternal joy. You know all our deeds.
Deliver us from evil, we that bow
And pray again and again. ⊕

Holding to the Constant

Break into the peace within,
Hold attention in stillness,
And in the world outside
You will ably master the ten thousand things.

All things rise and flourish
Then go back to their roots.
Seeing this return brings true rest,
Where you discover who you really are.
Knowing who you are, you will find the constant.
Those who lack harmony with the constant court danger,
But those who have it gain new vision.

They act with compassion;
    within themselves, they can find room for everything.
Having room, they rule themselves and lead others wisely.
Being wise, they live in accordance
    with the nature of things.
Emptied of self and one with nature,
They become filled with the Tao.
The Tao endures forever.
For those who have attained harmony with the Tao
    will never lose it,
Even if their bodies die. ✦

Radiant Is the World Soul

Radiant is the world soul,
Full of splendor and beauty,
Full of life,
Of souls hidden,
Of treasures of the holy spirit,
Of fountains of strength,
Of greatness and beauty.
Proudly I ascend
Toward the heights of the world soul
That gives life to the universe.
How majestic the vision –
Come, enjoy,
Come, find peace,
Embrace delight,
Taste and see that God is good.
Why spend your substance on what does not nourish
And your labor on what cannot satisfy?
Listen to me, and you will enjoy what is good,
And find delight in what is truly precious. ✧

The Path of Love

O seeker of truth, it is your heart's eye you must open.
Know the Divine Unity today,
> through the path of love for Him.

If you object:
"I am waiting for my mind to grasp His nature,"
Know the Divine Unity today,
> through the path of love for Him.

Should you wish to behold the face of God,
Surrender to Him, and invoke His names.

When your soul is clear, a light of true joy shall shine.
Know the Divine Unity today,
> through the path of love for Him. ⊷

Let Nothing Upset You

Let nothing upset you;
Let nothing frighten you.
Everything is changing;
God alone is changeless.
Patience attains the goal.
Who has God lacks nothing;
God alone fills every need. ↷

Twin Verses

All that we are is the result of what we have thought: we are formed and molded by our thoughts. Those whose minds are shaped by selfish thoughts cause misery when they speak or act. Sorrows roll over them as the wheels of a cart roll over the tracks of the bullock that draws it.

All that we are is the result of what we have thought: we are formed and molded by our thoughts. Those whose minds are shaped by selfless thoughts give joy whenever they speak or act. Joy follows them like a shadow that never leaves them.

"He insulted me, he struck me, he cheated me, he robbed me": those caught in resentful thoughts never find peace.

"He insulted me, he struck me, he cheated me, he robbed me": those who give up resentful thoughts surely find peace.

For hatred does not cease by hatred at any time: hatred ceases by love. This is an unalterable law.

There are those who forget that death will come to all. For those who remember, quarrels come to an end.

Those who live only for pleasure, who eat intemperately, who are lazy and weak and lack control over their senses, are like a tree with shallow roots. As a strong wind uproots such a tree, Mara the Tempter will throw such a person down.

But those who live without looking for pleasure, who eat temperately and control their senses, who are persevering and firm in faith, are like a mountain. As a strong wind cannot uproot a mountain, Mara cannot throw such a person down.

Whoever puts on the saffron robe but is self-willed, speaks untruthfully, and lacks self-control is not worthy of that sacred garment.

But those who have vanquished self-will, who speak the truth and have mastered themselves, are firmly established on the spiritual path and worthy of the saffron robe.

The deluded, imagining trivial things to be vital to life, follow their vain fancies and never attain the highest knowledge. But the wise, knowing what is trivial and what is vital, set their thoughts on the supreme goal and attain the highest knowledge.

As rain seeps through a poorly thatched roof, passion seeps into the untrained mind. As rain cannot seep through a well-thatched roof, passion cannot seep into a well-trained mind.

Those who are selfish suffer here and suffer there; they suffer wherever they go. They suffer and fret over the damage they have done.

But those who are selfless rejoice here and rejoice there; they rejoice wherever they go. They rejoice and delight in the good they have done.

The selfish person suffers here, and he suffers there; he suffers wherever he goes. He suffers as he broods over the damage he has done. He suffers more and more as he travels along the path of sorrow.

The selfless person is happy here, and he is happy there; he is happy wherever he goes. He is happy when he thinks of the good he has done. He grows in happiness as he progresses along the path of bliss.

Those who recite many scriptures but do not practice their teachings are like a cowherd counting another's cows. They do not share in the joys of the spiritual life.

But those who may know few scriptures but practice their teachings, who overcome all lust, hatred, and delusion, live with a pure mind in the highest wisdom. They stand without external supports and share in the joys of the spiritual life. ☙

I Know That He Reveals Himself

I sit alone apart from all the world
    and see before me Him who transcends the world.
I see Him and He sees me;
I love Him and I believe that He loves me;
I am nourished and satisfied only with His vision.
United with Him I go beyond heaven.
All this I know beyond any doubt,
    but where my body is I do not know.

I know that He who is immovable descends;
I know that He who is invisible appears to me;
I know that He who transcends all creation
    takes me into Himself and hides me in His arms
    apart from all the world;
and then I, small and mortal in this world,
    I see the Creator of the world within me
and know that I can never die
    because I am within all life
    and all of life wells up in me.
He is in my heart, He is in heaven;
    both here and there He reveals Himself to me
    in equal glory. ⟡

Cast Aside What Limits You

The human body is finite;
>the spirit is boundless.
Before you begin to pray,
>cast aside what limits you
>and enter into the world of the Infinite.
Turn to God alone
>and have no thought of self at all.
Nothing but God will exist for you
>when self has ceased to be. ✦

The Way of Love

ARJUNA:

Of those who love you as the Lord of Love,
Ever present in all, and those who seek you
As the nameless, formless Reality,
Which way is sure and swift, love or knowledge?

SRI KRISHNA:

For those who set their hearts on me
And worship me with unfailing devotion and faith,
The way of love leads sure and swift to me.

Those who seek the transcendental Reality,
Unmanifested, without name or form,
Beyond the reach of feeling and of thought,
With their senses subdued and mind serene
And striving for the good of all beings,
They too will verily come unto me.

                                        Yet hazardous
And slow is the path to the Unrevealed,
Difficult for physical man to tread.
But they for whom I am the goal supreme,
Who do all work renouncing self for me
And meditate on me with single-hearted
Devotion, these will I swiftly rescue

From the fragment's cycle of birth and death
To fullness of eternal life in me.

Still your mind in me, still yourself in me,
And without doubt you shall be united with me,
Lord of Love, dwelling in your heart.
But if you cannot still your mind in me,
Learn to do so through the practice of meditation.
If you lack the will for such self-discipline,
Engage yourself in selfless service of all around you,
For selfless service can lead you at last to me.
If you are unable to do even this,
Surrender yourself to me in love,
Receiving success and failure with equal calmness
As granted by me.

Better indeed is knowledge than mechanical practice.
Better than knowledge is meditation.
But better still is surrender in love,
Because there follows immediate peace.

That one I love who is incapable of ill will,
And returns love for hatred.
Living beyond the reach of I and *mine*
And of pleasure and pain, full of mercy,
Contented, self-controlled, firm in faith,
With all his heart and all his mind given
To me –with such a one I am in love.

Not agitating the world or by it agitated,
They stand above the sway of elation,
Competition, and fear, accepting life
Good and bad as it comes. They are pure,
Efficient, detached, ready to meet every demand
I make on them as humble instruments of my work.

They are dear to me who run not after the pleasant
Or away from the painful, grieve not
Over the past, lust not today,
But let things come and go as they happen.

Who serve both friend and foe with equal love,
Not buoyed up by praise or cast down by blame,
Alike in heat and cold, pleasure and pain,
Free from selfish attachments and self-will,
Ever full, in harmony everywhere,
Firm in faith – such as these are dear to me.

But dearest to me are those who seek me
In faith and love as life's eternal goal.
They go beyond death to immortality. ✑

The Beatitudes

Blessed are the poor in spirit:

   for theirs is the kingdom of heaven.

Blessed are they that mourn:

   for they shall be comforted.

Blessed are the meek:

   for they shall inherit the earth.

Blessed are they which do hunger and thirst

   after righteousness:

   for they shall be filled.

Blessed are the merciful:

   for they shall obtain mercy.

Blessed are the pure in heart:

   for they shall see God.

Blessed are the peacemakers:

   for they shall be called the children of God.

Blessed are they which are persecuted

   for righteousness' sake:

   for theirs is the kingdom of heaven.

Blessed are ye, when men shall revile you, and persecute
you, and shall say all manner of evil against you falsely,
for my sake. Rejoice, and be exceeding glad: for great is
your reward in heaven: for so persecuted they the prophets
which were before you.

Ye are the salt of the earth: but if the salt have lost its savor, wherewith shall it be salted? It is thenceforth good for nothing, but to be cast out, and to be trodden under foot of men.

Ye are the light of the world. A city that is set on a hill cannot be hid. Neither do men light a candle, and put it under a bushel, but on a candlestick; and it giveth light unto all that are in the house. Let your light so shine before men, that they may see your good works, and glorify your Father which is in heaven.

The Unstruck Bells & Drums

The Lord is in me, the Lord is in you,
    as life is in every seed.
O servant! Put false pride away
    and seek for him within you.
A million suns are ablaze with light,
The sea of blue spreads in the sky,
The fever of life is stilled, and all stains
    are washed away
When I sit in the midst of that world.

Hark to the unstruck bells and drums!
Take your delight in love!
Rains pour down without water,
    and the rivers are streams of light.
One love it is that pervades the whole world;
    few there are who know it fully:
They are blind who hope to see it by the light of reason,
    that reason which is the cause of separation –
The house of reason is very far away!

How blessed is Kabir, that amidst this great joy
    he sings within his own vessel.
It is the music of the meeting of soul with soul;

It is the music of the forgetting of sorrows;
It is the music that transcends all coming in
and all going forth. ⊹

The Wonderful Effect of Divine Love

1

Ah, Lord God, thou holy lover of my soul, when thou comest into my heart, all that is within me shall rejoice. Thou art my glory and the exultation of my heart: thou art my hope and refuge in the day of my trouble.

2

But because I am as yet weak in love, and imperfect in virtue, I have need to be strengthened and comforted by thee; visit me therefore often, and instruct me with all holy discipline.

Set me free from evil passions, and heal my heart of all inordinate affections; that being inwardly cured and thoroughly cleansed, I may be made fit to love, courageous to suffer, steady to persevere.

3

Love is a great thing, yea, a great and thorough good; by itself it makes every thing that is heavy, light; and it bears evenly all that is uneven. For it carries a burden which is no burden, and makes every thing that is bitter, sweet and tasteful. The noble love of Jesus impels one to do great things, and stirs one up to be always longing for what is more perfect.

Love desires to be aloft, and will not be kept back by any thing low and mean.

Love desires to be free, and estranged from all worldly affections, that so its inward sight may not be hindered; that it may not be entangled by any temporal prosperity, or by any adversity subdued.

Nothing is sweeter than love, nothing more courageous, nothing higher, nothing wider, nothing more pleasant, nothing fuller nor better in heaven and earth; because love is born of God, and cannot rest but in God, above all created things.

4

He that loveth, flyeth, runneth, and rejoiceth; he is free, and cannot be held in. He giveth all for all, and hath all in all; because he resteth in One highest above all things, from whom all that is good flows and proceeds.

He respecteth not the gifts, but turneth himself above all goods unto the Giver.

Love often times knoweth no measure, but is fervent beyond all measure. Love feels no burden, thinks nothing of trouble, attempts what is above its strength, pleads no excuse of impossibility; for it thinks all things lawful for itself and all things possible. It is therefore able to undertake all things, and it completes many things, and warrants them to take effect, where he who does not love would faint and lie down.

5

Love is watchful, and sleeping slumbereth not. Though weary, it is not tired; though pressed, it is not straitened; though alarmed, it is not confounded; but as a lively flame and burning torch, it forces its way upwards, and securely passes through all.

If any one love, he knoweth what is the cry of this voice. For it is a loud cry in the ears of God, the mere ardent affection of the soul, when it saith, "My God, my love, thou art all mine, and I am all thine."

6

Enlarge thou me in love, that with the inward palate of my heart I may taste how sweet it is to love, and to be dissolved, and as it were to bathe myself in thy love.

Let me be possessed by love, mounting above myself, through excessive fervor and admiration.

Let me sing the song of love, let me follow thee, my Beloved, on high; let my soul spend itself in thy praise, rejoicing through love.

Let me love thee more than myself, nor love myself but for thee: and in thee all that truly love thee, as the law of love commandeth, shining out from thyself.

7

Love is active, sincere, affectionate, pleasant and amiable; courageous, patient, faithful, prudent, long-suffering, resolute, and never seeking itself. For in whatever instance one seeketh oneself, there he falleth from love.

Love is circumspect, humble, and upright: not yielding to softness, or to levity, nor attending to vain things; it is sober, chaste, steady, quiet, and guarded in all the senses.

Love is subject, and obedient to its superiors, to itself mean and despised, unto God devout and thankful, trusting and hoping always in Him, even then when God imparteth no relish of sweetness unto it: for without sorrow, none liveth in love.

8

He that is not prepared to suffer all things, and to stand to the will of his Beloved, is not worthy to be called a lover of God. A lover ought to embrace willingly all that is hard and distasteful, for the sake of his Beloved; and not to turn away from him for any contrary accidents. ⊷

Prayer for Peace

Adorable presence,
Thou who art within and without,
    above and below and all around,
Thou who art interpenetrating
    every cell of my being,
Thou who art the eye of my eyes,
    the ear of my ears,
    the heart of my heart,
    the mind of my mind,
    the breath of my breath,
    the life of my life,
    the soul of my soul,
Bless us, dear God, to be aware of thy presence
    now and here.

May we all be aware of thy presence
    in the East and the West,
    in the North and the South.
May peace and good will abide among individuals,
    communities, and nations. ❧

Dawn Prayer

O God, the night has passed and the day has dawned.
How I long to know if Thou hast accepted my prayers
    or if Thou hast rejected them. Therefore console me,
    for it is Thine to console this state of mine.
Thou hast given me life and cared for me
    and Thine is the glory. If Thou wert to drive me from
    Thy door, yet would I not forsake it, for the love
    that I bear in my heart for Thee.

O my Joy and my Desire and my Refuge,
    my Friend and my Sustainer and my Goal,
    Thou art my Intimate, and longing for Thee sustains me.
Were it not for Thee, O my Life and my Friend,
    how I should have been distraught
    over the spaces of the earth!

How many favors have been bestowed,
    and how much hast Thou given me
    Of gifts and grace and assistance.
Thy love is now my desire and my bliss,
    and has been revealed to the eye of my heart
    that was athirst. ⬦

Beloved of the Soul

Beloved of the soul, source of compassion,
Shape your servant to your will.
Then your servant will run like a deer to bow before you.
Your love will be sweeter than a honeycomb.
Majestic, beautiful, light of the universe,
My soul is lovesick for you;
I implore you, God, heal her
By revealing to her your pleasant radiance;
Then she will be strengthened and healed
And will have eternal joy.
Timeless One, be compassionate
And have mercy on the one you love,
For this is my deepest desire:
To see your magnificent splendor.
This is what my heart longs for;
Have mercy and do not conceal yourself.
Reveal yourself, my Beloved,
And spread the shelter of your peace over me;
Light up the world with your glory;
We will celebrate you in joy.
Hurry, Beloved, the time has come,
And grant us grace, as in days of old. ❧

The Lord Is My Shepherd

The Lord is my shepherd; I shall not want.

He maketh me to lie down in green pastures;
    He leadeth me beside the still waters.

He restoreth my soul; He guideth me in straight paths
    for His name's sake.

Yea, though I walk through the valley
    of the shadow of death,
    I will fear no evil, for Thou art with me;
    Thy rod and Thy staff, they comfort me.

Thou preparest a table before me
    in the presence of mine enemies;
    Thou hast anointed my head with oil;
    my cup runneth over.

Surely goodness and mercy shall follow me
    all the days of my life;
    and I shall dwell in the house of the Lord forever.

Discourse on Good Will

May all beings be filled with joy and peace.
May all beings everywhere,
The strong and the weak,
The great and the small,
The mean and the powerful,
The short and the long,
The subtle and the gross –

May all beings everywhere,
Seen and unseen,
Dwelling far off or nearby,
Being or waiting to become,
May all be filled with lasting joy.

Let no one deceive another,
Let no one anywhere despise another,
Let no one out of anger or resentment
Wish suffering on anyone at all.

Just as a mother with her own life
Protects her child, her only child, from harm,
So within yourself let grow
A boundless love for all creatures.

Let your love flow outward through the universe,
To its height, its depth, its broad extent,
A limitless love, without hatred or enmity.

Then, as you stand or walk,
Sit or lie down,
As long as you are awake,
Strive for this with a one-pointed mind;
Your life will bring heaven to earth. ↢

Invocations

In the name of God,
Most gracious,
Most merciful.

O thou munificent one
Who art the bestower of all bounties,
O thou wise one
Who overlookest our faults,
O self-existent one
Who art beyond our comprehension,
O thou omnipotent one
Who hast no equal in power and greatness,
Who art without a second:
O thou merciful one
Who guidest stray souls to the right path,
Thou art truly our God.

Give purity to our minds,
Aspiration to our hearts,
Light to our eyes.
Out of thy grace and bounty
Give us that which thou deemest best.

O Lord, out of thy grace
Give faith and light to our hearts,
And with the medicine of truth and steadfastness
Cure the ills of this life.
I know not what to ask of thee.
Thou art the knower;
Give what thou deemest best.

O God, may my brain reel with thoughts of thee,
May my heart thrill with the mysteries of thy grace,
May my tongue move only to utter thy praise.

I live only to do thy will;
My lips move only in praise of thee.
O Lord, whoever becometh aware of thee,
Casteth out all else other than thee.

O Lord, give me a heart
That I may pour it out in thanksgiving.
Give me life
That I may spend it in working
For the salvation of the world.

O Lord, give me that right discrimination
That the lure of the world may cheat me no more.
Give me strength
That my faith suffer no eclipse.

O Lord, give me understanding
That I stray not from the path.
Give me light
To avoid pitfalls.

O Lord, keep watch over me
That I stray not.
Keep me on the path of righteousness
That I escape from the pangs of repentance.

O Lord, judge me not by my actions.
Of thy mercy, save me,
And make my humble efforts fruitful.

O Lord, give me a heart
Free from the flames of desire.
Give me a mind
Free from the waves of egoism.
O Lord, give me eyes
Which see nothing but thy glory.
Give me a mind
That finds delight in thy service.
Give me a soul
Drunk in the wine of thy wisdom.

O Lord, to find thee is my desire,
But to comprehend thee is beyond my strength.

Remembering thee is solace to my sorrowing heart;
Thoughts of thee are my constant companions.
I call upon thee night and day.
The flame of thy love glows
In the darkness of my night.

Life in my body pulsates only for thee,
My heart beats in resignation to thy will.
If on my dust a tuft of grass were to grow,
Every blade would tremble with my devotion for thee.

O Lord, everyone desires to behold thee.
I desire that thou mayest cast a glance at me.
Let me not disgrace myself.
If thy forgiveness awaits me in the end,
Lower not the standard of forgiveness
Which thou hast unfurled.

O Lord, prayer at thy gate
Is a mere formality:
Thou knowest what thy slave desires.
O Lord, better for me to be dust
And my name effaced
From the records of the world
Than that thou forget me.

He knoweth all our good and evil.
Nothing is hidden from him.

He knoweth what is the best medicine
To cure the pain and to rescue the fallen.
Be humble, for he exalteth the humble.
I am intoxicated with love for thee
And need no fermented wine.
I am thy bird, free from need of seed
And safe from the snare of the fowler.
In the kaaba and in the temple,
Thou art the object of my search,
Else I am freed
From both these places of worship.

Lord, when thou wert hidden from me
The fever of life possessed me.
When thou revealest thyself
This fever of life departeth.

O Lord, other men are afraid of thee
But I – I am afraid of myself.
From thee flows good alone,
From me flows evil.
Others fear what the morrow may bring;
I am afraid of what happened yesterday.

O Lord, if thou holdest me responsible for my sins
I shall cling to thee for thy grace.
I with my sin am an insignificant atom.
Thy grace is resplendent as the sun.

O Lord, out of regard for thy name,

The qualities which are thine,

Out of regard for thy greatness,

Listen to my cry,

For thou alone canst redeem me.

O Lord, intoxicate me with the wine of thy love.

Place the chains of thy slavery on my feet;

Make me empty of all but thy love,

And in it destroy me and bring me back to life.

The hunger thou has awakened

Culminates in fulfillment.

Make my body impervious to the fires of hell;

Vouchsafe to me a vision of thee in heaven.

The spark thou hast kindled, make it everlasting.

I think of no other,

And in thy love care for none else.

None has a place in my heart but thee.

My heart has become thine abode;

It has no place for another.

O Lord, thou cherishest the helpless,

And I am helpless.

Apply thy balm to my bleeding heart,

For thou art the physician.

O Lord, I, a beggar, ask of thee
More than what a thousand kings may ask of thee.
Each one has something he needs to ask of thee;
I have come to ask thee to give me thyself.
If words can establish a claim,
I claim a crown.
But if deeds are wanted,
I am as helpless as the ant.

Urged by desire, I wandered
In the streets of good and evil.
I gained nothing except feeding the fire of desire.
As long as in me remains the breath of life,
Help me, for thou alone canst hear my prayer.

Watch vigilantly the state of thine own mind.
Love of God begins in harmlessness.

Know that the prophet built an external *kaaba*
Of clay and water
And an inner *kaaba* in life and heart.
The outer *kaaba* was built by Abraham, the holy;
The inner is sanctified by the glory of God himself.

On the path of God
Two places of worship mark the stages,

The material temple
And the temple of the heart.
Make your best endeavor
To worship at the temple of the heart.

In this path, be one
With a heart full of compassion.
Engage not in vain doing;
Make not thy home in the street of lust and desire.
If thou wouldst become a pilgrim on the path of love,
The first condition is that thou become
As humble as dust and ashes.

Know that when thou learnest to lose thy self
Thou wilt reach the Beloved.
There is no other secret to be revealed,
And more than this is not known to me.

Be humble and cultivate silence.
If thou hast received, rejoice,
And fill thyself with ecstasy.
And if not, continue the demand.

What is worship?
To realize reality.
What is the sacred law?
To do no evil.

What is reality?
Selflessness.

The heart inquired of the soul,
What is the beginning of this business?
What its end, and what its fruit?
The soul answered:
The beginning of it is the annihilation of self,
Its end faithfulness,
And its fruit immortality.

The heart asked, what is annihilation?
What is faithfulness?
What is immortality?
The soul answered:
Freedom from self is annihilation.
Faithfulness is fulfillment of love.
Immortality is the union of immortal with mortal.

In this path the eye must cease to see
And the ear to hear,
Save unto him and about him.
Be as dust on his path;
Even the kings of this earth
Make the dust of his feet
The balm of their eyes. ⟡

Whatever You Do

A leaf, a flower, a fruit, or even
Water, offered to me in devotion,
I will accept as the loving gift
Of a dedicated heart. Whatever you do,
Make it an offering to me –
The food you eat or worship you perform,
The help you give, even your suffering.
Thus will you be free from karma's bondage,
From the results of action, good and bad.

I am the same to all beings. My love
Is the same always. Nevertheless, those
Who meditate on me with devotion,
They dwell in me, and I shine forth in them.

Even the worst sinner becomes a saint
When he loves me with all his heart. This love
Will soon transform his personality
And fill his heart with peace profound.
O son of Kunti, this is my promise:
Those who love me, they shall never perish.

Even those who are handicapped by birth
Have reached the supreme goal in life
By taking refuge in me. How much more
The pure brahmins and royal sages who love me!

Give not your love to this transient world
Of suffering, but give all your love to me.
Give me your mind, your heart, all your worship.
Long for me always, live for me always,
And you shall be united with me. ✦

Practicing the Presence of God

1

O my God, since thou art with me, and I must now, in obedience to thy commands, apply my mind to these outward things, I beseech thee to grant me the grace to continue in thy presence; and to this end do thou prosper me with thy assistance, receive all my works, and possess all my affections.

2

God knoweth best what is needful for us, and all that he does is for our good. If we knew how much he loves us, we should always be ready to receive equally and with indifference from his hand the sweet and the bitter. All would please that came from him. The sorest afflictions never appear intolerable, except when we see them in the wrong light. When we see them as dispensed by the hand of God, when we know that it is our loving Father who abases and distresses us, our sufferings will lose their bitterness and become even matter of consolation.

Let all our employment be to know God; the more one knows him, the more one desires to know him. And as knowledge is commonly the measure of love, the deeper and more extensive our knowledge shall be, the greater will be our love; and if our love of God were great, we should love him equally in pains and pleasures.

Let us not content ourselves with loving God for the mere sensible favors, how elevated soever, which he has done or may do us. Such favors, though never so great, cannot bring us so near to him as faith does in one simple act. Let us seek him often by faith. He is within us; seek him not elsewhere. If we do love him alone, are we not rude, and do we not deserve blame, if we busy ourselves about trifles which do not please and perhaps offend him? It is to be feared these trifles will one day cost us dear.

Let us begin to be devoted to him in good earnest. Let us cast everything besides out of our hearts. He would possess them alone. Beg this favor of him. If we do what we can on our part, we shall soon see that change wrought in us which we aspire after. ↭

The Miracle of Illumination

As a blind man feels when he finds a pearl
    in a dustbin, so am I amazed by the miracle
    of Bodhi rising in my consciousness.
It is the nectar of immortality that delivers us from death,
The treasure that lifts us above poverty into
    the wealth of giving to life,
The tree that gives shade to us when we roam about
    scorched by life,
The bridge that takes us across the stormy river of life,
The cool moon of compassion that calms our mind
    when it is agitated,
The sun that dispels darkness,
The butter made from the milk of kindness
    by churning it with the dharma.
It is a feast of joy to which all are invited. ❧

I Am the One Who Will Never Forget You

How blessed are those whose way is pure,
>Who walk along the path you have shown them.
How blessed are those who hear your voice,
>who seek your care with all their hearts.
I pray that my ways please you,
>that they be set according to your ways.

My soul cleaves to the dust;
>my eyes stare into the night.
O giver of life!
I have prayed, and you have answered;
I have wept, and you have given me strength.
O Lord, remove the darkness from my soul
>and show me the light of your truth.

May your love and kindness find shelter
>in the depths of my heart.
May your word be my salvation.
O Lord, do not take the truth from my lips,
>keep it with me
>so I may sing your glory forever.

I will walk freely, speaking to all who seek your wisdom;
I will tell of your miracle to kings and princes,
       and I will not be daunted.
I will delight in your wisdom,
I will reach out my hand for your touch,
       and I will hold on to your every word.
How great is my fortune,
How great are the gifts that come from you.

Your hands made me and fashioned me;
       show me the truth,
       and the wisdom to know your will.
Let the people who love you see me and be glad;
       for they will know that I am your messenger,
       that I come to speak your words.

O Lord, I know that every hardship along the way
       is for me to grow in your love.
May I find delight in all you give me,
May I comfort all those who turn in my direction,
May my joy be complete
       and your Name forever on my lips.

My soul longs to know you again;
I stand here hoping for a sign,
       hoping for a thread to hang on to . . .
My sight has grown dim searching for you.
When will you come?

When will you show yourself to me?
I may shrivel up like a wineskin,
I may be hounded by countless lies,
I may be swept from the face of this earth,
>   but I will never turn away from you.
What was I born for if not to follow you?
What is there to live for if not your undying love?
O Lord come alive in my heart—
Come alive so that we may,
>   once again,
>   be as one.

O Lord, your Word is eternal.
It is fixed in the heavens,
It stands as firm as the earth.
It has fulfilled the prayers of every generation.
O Lord, without the strength that comes
>   from your Name,
>   I surely would have perished long ago.

I will never forget your teachings,
>   for through them you have come alive within me.
I may see the heavens fall,
I may see the earth crumble,
I may see all creation come to an end,
>   but I will stand, forever here,
>   as your servant.

O Lord, I hold your love with me all the time.
It makes me strong,
It cuts through my doubts,
It gives me great insight
        and the wisdom of a sage,
It keeps me on the right path.
How sweet is your love to my taste,
        sweeter than honey to my lips!
O Lord what is there without your love?
Without your love there is nothing
        but the taste of bitterness.

O Lord, you are a lamp to my feet,
        a light on my path.
Wherever you go, there I have sworn to follow.
I know the way may be steep
        and the journey filled with pain,
        but every step of the way
        you will give me strength.
O Lord, how can I ever hope to repay you?
All I can offer is folded hands
        and the readiness to do as you bid me.
You are my everlasting inheritance;
        you are the joy of my life.
I stand here resolved, to do as you command,
I follow the path
        that leads me back to you.

Thou art my shield and my hiding place.

Thou art my sole protector.

Thou art my only support.

O Lord, banish all evil from my mind

and replace it with the yearning to know you.

Give me faith and humility

and keep me free from harm.

What use is this life without you?

You are all that is safe,

you are all that is true.

All my life I have looked for you.

Could you let these eyes fail

before they have rested upon your form?

Could you forsake me that way?

O Lord, be kind to your servant –

show yourself to me.

This is my truth, this is my life,

this is what I want more

than all the world has to offer.

Every word that comes from your lips

fills me with wonder.

And here I sit, waiting to do as you bid me.

Your words shine;

they illumine those in despair;

they give understanding to the simple.

I am out of breath calling for you. . . .

Turn in my direction

> and fill me with your grace.

I am knocking – answer:

> for this is the promise

> you have given to all those who love you.

O Lord, fulfill your promise –

> keep my feet on the path that leads to your glory.

Do not let anything take me away.

Let the glory of your splendor

> be seen by this servant of yours . . .

If I go my own way

> and do not follow your laws

> then let me suffer,

> let me wail,

> let my eyes run down with a flood of tears.

I cry out with my whole heart – answer me, O Lord!

Save me, from this ocean of darkness.

Show me the way out.

I rise before dawn and wait to hear your voice.

My eyes stay open past the midnight watch,

> so that I might come to know all you have taught me.

You are so near, my Lord;

> you are the eternal support;

> you are the Supreme goal . . .

I have but one prayer:

> that every step I take
> be a step toward you.

My heart stands in awe of you,

> and I am filled with joy whenever I hear your Name.

Seven times a day I praise thee;

> seven times a day I remember the justice of your care.

Those who love everything you give,

> find great peace,
> and nothing causes them to stumble.

Here I am, do with me as you will,

> for all my life lies open before thee.

Let these tears of mine reach you,

> let these supplications be seen by you.

Let my tongue sing of your glory,

> and let my life be a testimony of your kindness . . .

O Lord, where is my salvation?
Where is this life bringing me?
If I go astray like a lost sheep, look for me.
Look for me O Lord!
For I am your servant;

> I am the one who will never forget you,
> I am the one who will never forget your love. ✑

The Whole World Is Your Own

I tell you one thing –
If you want peace of mind,
    do not find fault with others.

Rather learn to see your own faults.
Learn to make the whole world your own.

No one is a stranger, my child;
    this whole world is your own. ↭

Epistle on Love

If I speak in the tongues of men and of angels, but have not love,
I am a noisy gong or a clanging cymbal. And if I have prophetic
powers, and understand all mysteries and all knowledge, and
if I have all faith, so as to remove mountains, but have not love,
I am nothing. If I give away all I have, and if I deliver my body
to be burned, but have not love, I gain nothing.

Love is patient and kind; love is not jealous or boastful; it is not
arrogant or rude. Love does not insist on its own way; it is not
irritable or resentful; it does not rejoice at wrong, but rejoices
in the right. Love bears all things, believes all things, hopes all
things, endures all things.

Love never ends; as for prophecies, they will pass away; as
for tongues, they will cease; as for knowledge, it will pass away.
For our knowledge is imperfect and our prophecy is imperfect;
but when the perfect comes, the imperfect will pass away.

When I was a child, I spoke like a child, I thought like a
child, I reasoned like a child; when I became a man, I gave
up childish ways. For now we see in a mirror dimly, but then
face to face. Now I know in part; then I shall understand fully,
even as I have been fully understood.

So faith, hope, love abide, these three;
but the greatest of these is love. ☙

What Is Real Never Ceases

The Self dwells in the house of the body,
Which passes through childhood, youth, and old age.
So passes the Self at the time of death
Into another body. The wise know this truth
And are not deceived by it.

When the senses come in contact with sense-objects
They give rise to feelings of heat and cold,
Pleasure and pain, which come and go.
Accept them calmly, as do the wise.

The wise, who live free from pleasure and pain,
Are worthy of immortality.

What is real never ceases to be.
The unreal never is. The sages
Who realize the Self know the secret
Of what is and what is not.

Know that the Self, the ground of existence,
Can never be destroyed or diminished.
For the changeless cannot be changed.

Bodies die, not the Self that dwells therein.
Know the Self to be beyond change and death.
Therefore strive to realize this Self.

Those who look upon the Self as slayer
Or as slain have not realized the Self.
How can the Self be killed or kill
When there is only One?

Never was the Self born; never shall it
Cease to be. Without beginning or end,
Free from birth, free from death, and free from time,
How can the Self die when the body dies?

Who knows the Self to be birthless, deathless,
Not subject to the tyranny of time,
How can the Self slay or cause to be slain?

Even as we cast off worn-out garments
And put on new ones, so casts off the Self
A worn-out body and enters into
Another that is new.

Not pierced by arrows nor burnt by fire,
Affected by neither water nor wind,
The Self is not a physical creature.

Not wounded, not burnt, not wetted, not dried,
The Self is ever and everywhere,
Immovable and everlasting.

The Self cannot be known by the senses,
Nor thought by the mind, nor caught by time.
If you know this, you will not grieve.

Even if you mistake the Self to be
Subject to birth and death, you must not grieve.
For death is certain for those who are born,
As rebirth is certain for those who die.
Why grieve over what cannot be avoided?

We perceive creatures only after birth,
And after they die we perceive them not.
They are manifest only between birth
And death. In this there is no cause for grief.

Some there are who have realized the Self
In all its wonder. Others can speak of it
As wonderful. But there are many
Who don't understand even when they hear.

Deathless is the Self in every creature.
Know this truth, and leave all sorrow behind. ৵

The Best

The best, like water,
Benefit all and do not compete.
They dwell in lowly spots that everyone else scorns.
Putting others before themselves,
They find themselves in the foremost place
And come very near to the Tao.
In their dwelling, they love the earth;
In their heart, they love what is deep;
In personal relationships, they love kindness;
In their words, they love truth.
In the world, they love peace.
In personal affairs, they love what is right.
In action, they love choosing the right time.
It is because they do not compete with others
That they are beyond the reproach of the world. ✧

Christ Be with Me

May the strength of God pilot me,
the power of God preserve me today.
May the wisdom of God instruct me,
the eye of God watch over me,
the ear of God hear me,
the word of God give me sweet talk,
the hand of God defend me,
the way of God guide me.

Christ be with me.
Christ before me.
Christ after me.
Christ in me.
Christ under me.
Christ over me.
Christ on my right hand.
Christ on my left hand.
Christ on this side.
Christ on that side.
Christ at my back.
Christ in the head of everyone to whom I speak.
Christ in the mouth of every person who speaks to me.
Christ in the eye of every person who looks at me.
Christ in the ear of every person who hears me today. ✤

Sabbath Prayer

Only for God doth my soul wait in stillness;
 from Him cometh my hope.
He alone is my rock and my salvation,
 I shall not be moved.
Show me Thy ways, O Lord; teach me Thy paths,
 guide me in Thy truth.
Whom have I in heaven but Thee? And having Thee
 I desire none else upon earth.
My flesh and my heart fail, but God is my strength
 and my portion forever.
Wait for the Lord, be strong, and let thy heart
 take courage.
Create in me a clean heart, O God;
 and renew a steadfast spirit within me.
When many cares perplex me, Thy comfort
 delights my soul.
My times are in Thy hand, and Thou wilt guide
 and sustain me even unto the end.
With Thee is the fountain of life;
In Thy light do we see light. ✧

Lord That Giveth Strength

1

My child, I am the Lord, that giveth strength in the day of tribulation. Come thou unto me, when it is not well with thee.

This is that which most of all hindereth heavenly consolation, that thou art too slow in turning thyself unto prayer.

For before thou dost earnestly supplicate me, thou seekest in the meanwhile many comforts, and refreshest thyself in outward things.

And hence it comes to pass that all doth little profit thee, until thou well consider that I am he who do rescue them that trust in me; and that out of me there is neither powerful help, nor profitable counsel, nor lasting remedy.

But do thou, having now recovered breath after the tempest, gather strength again in the light of my mercies; for I am at hand (saith the Lord) to repair all, not only entirely, but also abundantly and in most plentiful measure.

2

Is there anything hard to me? Or shall I be like one that saith and doeth not?

Where is thy faith? Stand firmly and with perseverance; take courage and be patient; comfort will come to thee in due time. Wait, wait, I say, for me: I will come and take care of thee. It is a temptation that vexeth thee, and a vain fear that affrighteth thee.

What else doth anxiety about future contingencies bring thee, but sorrow upon sorrow? Sufficient for the day is the evil thereof.

It is a vain thing and unprofitable to be either disturbed or pleased about future things, which perhaps will never come to pass.

3

But it is incident to man to be deluded with such imaginations; and a sign of a mind as yet weak to be so easily drawn away by the suggestions of the Enemy.

For so he may delude and deceive thee, he careth not whether it be by true or by false propositions; nor whether he over-throws thee with the love of present, or the fear of future things. Let not therefore thy heart be troubled, neither let it fear. Trust in me, and put thy confidence in my mercy.

When thou thinkest thyself farthest off from me, oftentimes I am nearest unto thee.

When thou countest almost all to be lost, then oftentimes the greatest gain of reward is close at hand. All is not lost, when any thing falleth out contrary.

Thou oughtest not to judge according to present feeling; nor so to take any grief, or give thyself over to it, from whencesoever it cometh, as though all hopes of escape were quite taken away.

4

Think not thyself wholly left, although for a time I have sent thee some tribulation, or even have withdrawn thy desired comfort; for this is the way to the kingdom of heaven.

And without doubt it is more expedient for thee and the rest of my servants that ye be exercised with adversities, than that ye should have all things according to your desires.

I know the secret thoughts of thy heart, and that it is very expedient for thy welfare that thou be left sometimes without taste (of spiritual sweetness, and in a dry condition), lest perhaps thou shouldest be puffed up with thy prosperous estate, and shouldest be willing to please thyself in that which thou art not.

That which I have given, I can take away; and I can restore it again when I please.

5

When I give it, it is mine; when I withdraw it, I take not
any thing that is thine; for mine is every good gift and every
perfect gift.

If I send upon thee affliction, or any cross whatever, repine
not, nor let thy heart fail thee; I can quickly succor thee, and
turn all thy heaviness into joy.

Howbeit I am righteous, and greatly to be praised when
I deal thus with thee.

6

If thou art wise, and considerest what the truth is, thou never
oughtest to mourn dejectedly for any adversity that befalleth
thee, but rather to rejoice and give thanks.

Yea, thou wilt account this time especial joy, that I afflict thee
with sorrows, and do not spare thee.

"As the Father hath loved me, I also love you," said I unto my
beloved disciples; whom certainly I sent not out to temporal
joys, but to great conflicts; not to honours, but to contempts;
not to idleness, but to labours; not to rest, but to bring forth
much fruit with patience. Remember thou these words,
O my child! ☙

The Mirror of This World

Every particle of the world is a mirror,
In each atom lies the blazing light
    of a thousand suns.
Cleave the heart of a raindrop,
    a hundred pure oceans will flow forth.
Look closely at a grain of sand,
    The seed of a thousand beings can be seen.
The foot of an ant is larger than an elephant;
In essence, a drop of water
    is no different than the Nile.
In the heart of a barley-corn
    lies the fruit of a hundred harvests;
Within the pulp of a millet seed
    an entire universe can be found.
In the wing of a fly, an ocean of wonder;
In the pupil of the eye, an endless heaven.
Though the inner chamber of the heart is small,
    the Lord of both worlds
    gladly makes his home there. ✺

Perennial Joy

THE KING OF DEATH

The joy of the spirit ever abides,
But not what seems pleasant to the senses.
Both these, differing in their purpose, prompt us
To action. All is well for those who choose
The joy of the spirit, but they miss
The goal of life who prefer the pleasant.
Perennial joy or passing pleasure?
This is the choice one is to make always.
The wise recognize this, but not
The ignorant. The first welcome what leads to joy
Abiding, even though painful at the time.
The latter run, goaded by their senses,
After what seems immediate pleasure.
Well have you renounced these passing pleasures
So dear to the senses, Nachiketa,
And turned your back on the way of the world
Which makes mankind forget the goal of life.

Far apart are wisdom and ignorance:
The first leads one to Self-realization;
The second makes one more and more
Estranged from one's real Self. I regard you,

Nachiketa, as worthy of instruction,
For passing pleasures tempt you not at all.

Ignorant of their ignorance, yet wise
In their own esteem, deluded people
Proud of their vain learning go round and round
Like the blind led by the blind. Far beyond
Their eyes, hypnotized by the world of sense,
Opens the way to immortality.
"I am my body; when my body dies,
I die." Living in this superstition they fall,
Life after life, under my sway.

It is but few who hear about the Self.
Fewer still dedicate their lives to its
Realization. Wonderful is the one
Who speaks of the Self. Rare are they
Who make it the supreme goal of their life.
Blessed are they who, through an illumined
Teacher, attain to Self-realization.
The truth of the Self cannot come through one
Who has not realized that he is the Self.
The intellect can never reach the Self,
Beyond its duality of subject
And object. He who sees himself in all
And all in him helps one through spiritual
Osmosis to realize the Self oneself.

This awakening you have known comes not
Through logic and scholarship, but from
Close association with a realized teacher.
Wise are you, Nachiketa, because you
Seek the Self eternal. May we have more
Seekers like you!

NACHIKETA

I know that earthly treasures are transient,
And never can I reach the Eternal
Through them. Hence have I renounced
All the desires of Nachiketa for earthly treasures
To win the Eternal through your instruction.

THE KING OF DEATH

I spread before your eyes, Nachiketa,
The fulfillment of all worldly desires:
Power to dominate the earth, delights
Celestial gained through religious rites, and
Miraculous powers beyond time and space.
These with will and wisdom have you renounced.

The wise, realizing through meditation
The timeless Self, beyond all perception,
Hidden in the cave of the heart,
Leave pain and pleasure far behind.
Those who know that they are neither body
Nor mind but the immemorial Self,

The divine principle of existence,
Find the source of all joy and live in joy
Abiding. I see the gates of joy
Are opening for you, Nachiketa.

NACHIKETA

Teach me of That you see as beyond right
And wrong, cause and effect, past and future.

THE KING OF DEATH

I will give you the Word all the scriptures
Glorify, all spiritual disciplines
Express, to attain which aspirants lead
A life of sense-restraint and self-naughting.
It is O M. This symbol of the Godhead
Is the highest. Realizing it, one finds
Complete fulfillment of all one's longings.
It is the greatest support to all seekers.
When O M reverberates unceasingly
Within one's heart, that one is indeed blessed
And greatly loved as one who is the Self.

The all-knowing Self was never born,
Nor will it die. Beyond cause and effect,
This Self is eternal and immutable.
When the body dies, the Self does not die.
If the slayer believes that he can kill

And the slain believes that he can be killed,
Neither knows the truth. The eternal Self
Slays not, nor is ever slain.

Hidden in the heart of every creature
Exists the Self, subtler than the subtlest,
Greater than the greatest. They go beyond
All sorrow who extinguish their self-will
And behold the glory of the Self
Through the grace of the Lord of Love.

Though one sits in meditation in a
Particular place, the Self within can
Exercise its influence far away.
Though still, it moves everything everywhere.

When the wise realize the Self, formless
In the midst of forms, changeless in the midst
Of change, omnipresent and supreme,
They go beyond all sorrow.

The Self cannot be known through the study
Of the scriptures, nor through the intellect,
Nor through hearing discourses about it.
It can be attained only by those
Whom the Self chooses. Verily unto them
Does the Self reveal itself.

The Self cannot be known by anyone
Who desists not from unrighteous ways,
Controls not the senses, stills not the mind,
And practices not meditation.

None else can know the omnipresent Self,
Whose glory sweeps away the rituals of
The priest and the prowess of the warrior
And puts death itself to death. ⊷

The Living God

Bow down before God, my precious thinking soul,
 and make haste to worship Him with reverence.

Night and day think only of your everlasting world.

Why should you chase after vanity and emptiness?

As long as you live, you are akin to the living God:
 just as He is invisible, so are you.

Since your Creator is pure and flawless,
 know that you too are pure and perfect.

The Mighty One upholds the heavens on His arm,
 as you uphold the mute body.

My soul, let your songs come before your Rock,
 who does not lay your form in the dust.

My innermost heart, bless your Rock always,
 whose name is praised by everything that has breath. ꙮ

A Sea of Peace

When the good God calls us in this world, he finds us full of vices and sins, and his first work is to give us the instinct to practice virtue; then he incites us to desire perfection, and afterwards, by infused grace, he conducts us to the true self-naughting, and finally to the true transformation. This is the extraordinary road along which God conducts the soul. But when the soul is thus naughted and transformed, it no longer works, or speaks, or wills, or feels, or understands, nor has it in itself any knowledge, either of that which is internal or external, which could possibly affect it; and, in all these things God is its director and guide without the help of any creature.

In this state, the soul is in such peace and tranquility that it seems to her that both soul and body are immersed in a sea of the profoundest peace, from which she would not issue for anything that could happen in this life. She remains immovable, imperturbable, and neither her humanity nor her spirit feels anything except the sweetest peace, of which she is so full that if her flesh, her bones, her nerves were pressed, nothing would issue from them but peace. And all day long she sings softly to herself for joy, saying: *"Shall I show thee what God is? No one finds peace apart from him."* ✦

You Are That

This is the teaching of Uddalaka to Shvetaketu, his son:

As by knowing one lump of clay, dear one,
We come to know all things made out of clay –
That they differ only in name and form,
While the stuff of which all are made is clay;

As by knowing one gold nugget, dear one,
We come to know all things made out of gold –
That they differ only in name and form,
While the stuff of which all are made is gold;

As by knowing one tool of iron, dear one,
We come to know all things made out of iron –
That they differ only in name and form,
While the stuff of which all are made is iron –

So through spiritual wisdom, dear one,
We come to know that all of life is one.

In the beginning was only Being,
One without a second.
Out of himself he brought forth the cosmos
And entered into everything in it.

There is nothing that does not come from him.
Of everything he is the inmost Self.
He is the truth; he is the Self supreme.
You are that, Shvetaketu; you are that.

When a person is absorbed in dreamless sleep
He is one with the Self, though he knows it not.
We say he sleeps, but he sleeps in the Self.

As a tethered bird grows tired of flying
About in vain to find a place of rest
And settles down at last on its own perch,
So the mind, tired of wandering about
Hither and thither, settles down at last
In the Self, dear one, to whom it is bound.

All creatures, dear one, have their source in him.
He is their home; he is their strength.
There is nothing that does not come from him.
Of everything he is the inmost Self.
He is the truth; he is the Self supreme.
You are that, Shvetaketu; you are that.

As bees suck nectar from many a flower
And make their honey one, so that no drop
Can say, "I am from this flower or that,"
All creatures, though one, know not they are that One.

There is nothing that does not come from him.
Of everything he is the inmost Self.
He is the truth; he is the Self supreme.
You are that, Shvetaketu; you are that.

As the rivers flowing east and west
Merge in the sea and become one with it,
Forgetting they were ever separate streams,
So do all creatures lose their separateness
When they merge at last into pure Being.
There is nothing that does not come from him.
Of everything he is the inmost Self.
He is the truth; he is the Self supreme.
You are that, Shvetaketu; you are that! ⟿

Cross the River Bravely

Cross the river bravely; conquer all your passions.
Go beyond the world of fragments and know the
deathless ground of life.

Cross the river bravely; conquer all your passions.
Go beyond your likes and dislikes and all fetters
will fall away.

Who is a true brahmin? That one I call a brahmin
who has neither likes nor dislikes and is free from
the chains of fear.

Who is a true brahmin? That one I call a brahmin
who has trained the mind to be still and reached the
supreme goal of life.

The sun shines in the day; the moon shines in the
night. The warrior shines in battle, the brahmin in
meditation. But day and night the Buddha shines
in radiance of love for all.

That one I call a brahmin who has shed all evil.
I call that one a recluse whose mind is serene;
a wanderer, whose heart is pure.

That one I call a brahmin who is never angry, never causes harm to others even when harmed by them.

That one I call a brahmin who clings not to pleasure. Do not cause sorrow to others; no more sorrow will come to you.

That one I call a brahmin who does not hurt others with unkind acts, words, or thoughts. Both body and mind obey him.

That one I call a brahmin who walks in the footsteps of the Buddha. Light your torch from the fire of his sacrifice.

It is not matted hair nor birth that makes a brahmin, but truth and the love for all of life with which one's heart is full.

What use is matted hair? What use is a deerskin on which to sit for meditation if your mind still seethes with lust?

Saffron robe and outward show do not make a brahmin, but training of the mind and senses through practice of meditation.

Neither riches nor high caste makes a brahmin. Free yourself from selfish desires and you will become a brahmin.

The brahmin has thrown off all chains and trembles not in fear. No selfish bonds can ensnare such a one, no impure thought pollute the mind.

That one I call a brahmin who has cut through the strap and thong and chain of karma. Such a one has got up from sleep, fully awake.

That one I call a brahmin who fears neither prison nor death. Such a one has the power of love no army can defeat.

That one I call a brahmin who is never angry, never goes astray from the path, who is pure and self-controlled. This body is the last.

That one I call a brahmin who clings not to pleasure, no more than water to a lotus leaf or mustard seed to the tip of a needle.

For such a one no more sorrow will come, no more burden will fall.

That one I call a brahmin whose wisdom is profound and whose understanding deep, who by following the right path and avoiding the wrong has reached the highest goal.

That one I call a brahmin whose wants are few, who is detached from householders and homeless mendicants alike.

That one I call a brahmin who has put aside weapons and renounced violence toward all creatures. Such a one neither kills nor helps others to kill.

That one I call a brahmin who is never hostile to those who are hostile toward him, who is detached among those who are selfish and at peace among those at war.

That one I call a brahmin from whom passion and hatred, arrogance and deceit, have fallen away like mustard seed from the point of a needle.

That one I call a brahmin who is ever true, ever kind. Such a one never asks what life can give, only 'What can I give life?'

That one I call a brahmin who has found his heaven, free from every selfish desire, free from every impurity.

Wanting nothing at all, doubting nothing at all, master of both body and mind, such a one has gone beyond time and death.

That one I call a brahmin who has gone beyond good and evil and is free from sorrow, passion, and impurity.

That one I call a brahmin who has risen above the duality of this world, free from sorrow and free from sin. Such a one shines like the full moon with no cloud in the sky.

That one I call a brahmin who has crossed the river difficult and dangerous to cross, and safely reached the other shore.

That one I call a brahmin who has turned his back upon himself. Homeless, such a one is ever at home; egoless, he is ever full.

Self-will has left his mind; it will never return. Sorrow has left his life; it will never return.

That one I call a brahmin who has overcome the urge to possess even heavenly things and is free from all selfish attachments.

That one I call a brahmin who is free from bondage to human beings and to nature alike, the hero who has conquered the world.

That one I call a brahmin who is free from *I, me,* and *mine,* who knows the rise and fall of life. Such a one is awake and will not fall asleep again.

That one I call a brahmin whose way no one can know. Such a one lives free from past and future, free from decay and death. Possessing nothing, desiring nothing for their own pleasure, their own profit, they have become a force for good, working for the freedom of all.

That one I call a brahmin who is fearless, heroic, unshakable,
a great sage who has conquered death and attained life's goal.

Brahmins have reached the end of the way; they have crossed
the river of life. All that they had to do is done: they have
become one with all life. ⊖

Do not look with fear
    on the changes and chances of this life;
    rather look to them with full faith that as they arise,
    God – whose you are – will deliver you out of them.
He has kept you hitherto.
Do not but hold fast to His dear hand,
    and He will lead you safely through all things;
    and when you cannot stand, He will bear you
    in His arms.
Do not anticipate what will happen tomorrow.
The same everlasting Father who cares for you today
    will take care of you tomorrow and every day.
Either He will shield you from suffering or
    He will give you unfailing strength to bear it.
Be at peace, then, and put aside all anxious thoughts
    and imaginations. ✣

Living in Wisdom

They live in wisdom
Who see themselves in all and all in them,
Whose love for the Lord of Love has consumed
Every selfish desire and sense craving
Tormenting the heart. Not agitated
By grief or hankering after pleasure,
They live free from lust and fear and anger.
Fettered no more by selfish attachments,
They are not elated by good fortune
Nor depressed by bad. Such are the seers.

Even as a tortoise draws in its limbs,
The wise can draw in their senses at will.
Aspirants abstain from sense pleasures,
But they still crave for them. These cravings all
Disappear when they see the Lord of Love.
For even of those who tread the path,
The stormy senses can sweep off the mind.
But they live in wisdom who subdue them
And keep their minds ever absorbed in me.

When you keep thinking about sense objects,
Attachment comes. Attachment breeds desire,
The lust of possession which, when thwarted,
Burns to anger. Anger clouds the judgment

And robs you of the power to learn from
Past mistakes. Lost is the discriminative
Faculty, and your life is utter waste.

But when you move amidst the world of sense
From both attachment and aversion freed,
There comes the peace in which all sorrows end,
And you live in the wisdom of the Self.

The disunited mind is far from wise;
How can it meditate? How be at peace?
When you know no peace, how can you know joy?
When you let your mind follow the Siren
Call of the senses, they carry away
Your better judgment as a cyclone drives
A boat off the charted course to its doom.

Use your mighty arms to free the senses
From attachment and aversion alike
And live in the full wisdom of the Self.
Such a sage awakes to light in the night
Of all creatures. In which they are awake
Is the night of ignorance to the sage.

As the rivers flow into the ocean
But cannot make the vast ocean overflow,

So flow the magic streams of the sense world
Into the sea of peace that is the sage.

They are forever free who have broken out
Of the ego-cage of *I* and *mine*
To be united with the Lord of Love.
This is the supreme state. Attain to this
And pass from death to immortality.↢

Great Life-Giving Spirit

Great Spirit of love, come to me with the power of the North.
Make me courageous when the cold winds of life fall upon me.
Give me strength and endurance for everything
    that is harsh, everything that hurts,
    everything that makes me squint.
Make me move through life
    ready to take what comes from the North.

Spirit who comes out of the East,
    come to me with the power of the rising sun.
Let there be light in my word.
Let there be light on the path that I walk.
Let me remember always that you give the gift of a new day.
Never let me be burdened with sorrow by not starting over.

Great Spirit of creation,
    send me the warm and soothing winds from the South.
Comfort me and caress me when I am tired and cold.
Enfold me as your gentle breezes enfold your leaves
    on the trees.
And as you give to all the earth your warm, moving wind,
Give to me so that I may grow close to you in warmth.

Great life-giving Spirit,
I face the West,
    the direction of the sundown.
Let me remember every day that the moment will come
    when my sun will go down.
Never let me forget that I must fade into you.
Give me beautiful color.
Give me a great sky for setting,
    and when it is time to meet you,
I come with glory.

And Giver of all life, I pray to you from the earth,
    help me to remember as I touch the earth
    that I am little and need your pity.
Help me to be thankful for the gift of the earth
    and never to walk hurtfully on the world.
Bless me to love what comes from mother earth
    and teach me how to love your gifts.

Great Spirit of the heavens,
    lift me up to you
    that my heart may worship you
    and come to you in glory.
Hold in my memory that you are my Creator,
    greater than I,
    eager for my good life.

Let everything that is in the world
    lift my mind,
    and my heart,
    and my life to you
    so that we may come always to you
    in truth and in heart. ✧

The Lord's Prayer

Our Father which art in heaven, hallowed be thy name.
Thy kingdom come,
Thy will be done in earth, as it is in heaven.
Give us this day our daily bread,
And forgive us our debts, as we forgive our debtors.
And lead us not into temptation, but deliver us from evil:
For thine is the kingdom, and the power,
     and the glory, for ever. ✧

The Path

I know the path: it is strait and narrow.
It is like the edge of a sword.
I rejoice to walk on it.
I weep when I slip.
God's word is:
"He who strives never perishes."
I have implicit faith in that promise.
Though, therefore, from my weakness
I fail a thousand times,
I shall not lose faith. ✧

Only God I Saw

In the market, in the cloister – only God I saw.
In the valley and on the mountain – only God I saw.

Him I have seen beside me oft in tribulation;
In favor and in fortune – only God I saw.

In prayer and fasting, in praise and contemplation,
In the religion of the Prophet – only God I saw.

Neither soul nor body, accident nor substance,
Qualities nor causes – only God I saw.

I oped mine eyes and by the light of his face around me
In all the eye discovered – only God I saw.

Like a candle I was melting in his fire:
Amidst the flames outflashing – only God I saw.

Myself with mine own eyes I saw most clearly,
But when I looked with God's eyes – only God I saw.

I passed away into nothingness, I vanished,
And lo, I was the All-living – only God I saw.

Lord, Thou Hast Searched Me

O Lord, Thou hast searched me, and known me.

Thou knowest my downsitting and mine uprising,
    Thou understandest my thought afar off.

Thou measurest my going about and my lying down,
    and art acquainted with all my ways.

For there is not a word in my tongue, but, lo, O Lord,
    Thou knowest it altogether.

Thou hast hemmed me in behind and before,
    and laid Thy hand upon me.

Such knowledge is too wonderful for me;
    too high, I cannot attain unto it.

Whither shall I go from Thy spirit?
    Or whither shall I flee from Thy presence?

If I ascend up into heaven, Thou art there;
    if I make my bed in the netherworld, behold,
    Thou art there.

If I take the wings of the morning,
and dwell in the uttermost parts of the sea;
Even there would Thy hand lead me,
and Thy right hand would hold me.
And if I say: "Surely the darkness shall envelop me,
and the light about me shall be night,"

Even the darkness is not too dark for Thee,
but the night shineth as the day;
the darkness is even as the light.

For Thou hast made my reins;
Thou hast knit me together in my mother's womb.

I will give thanks unto Thee,
for I am fearfully and wonderfully made;
wonderful are Thy works,
and that my soul knoweth right well.

My frame was not hidden from Thee
when I was made in secret
and curiously wrought in the lowest parts of the earth.

Thine eyes did see mine unformed substance,
and in Thy book they were all written –
even the days that were fashioned
when as yet there was none of them.

How weighty also are Thy thoughts unto me, O God!

    How great is the sum of them!

If I would count them,

    they are more in number than the sand;

Were I to come to the end of them,

    I would still be with Thee.

Search me, O God, and know my heart,

    try me, and know my thoughts;

And see if there be any way in me that is grievous,

    and lead me in the way everlasting. ✧

The City of Brahman

In the city of Brahman is a secret dwelling, the lotus of the heart. Within this dwelling is a space, and within that space is the fulfillment of our desires. What is within that space should be longed for and realized.

As great as the infinite space beyond is the space within the lotus of the heart. Both heaven and earth are contained in that inner space, both fire and air, sun and moon, lightning and stars. Whether we know it in this world or know it not, everything is contained in that inner space.

Never fear that old age will invade that city; never fear that this inner treasure of all reality will wither and decay. This knows no age when the body ages; this knows no dying when the body dies. This is the real city of Brahman; this is the Self, free from old age, from death and grief, hunger and thirst. In the Self all desires are fulfilled.

The Self desires only what is real, thinks nothing but what is true. Here people do what they are told, becoming dependent on their country, or their piece of land, or the desires of another, so their desires are not fulfilled and their works come to nothing, both in this world and in the next.

Those who depart from this world without knowing who they are or what they truly desire have no freedom here or hereafter.

But those who leave here knowing who they are and what they truly desire have freedom everywhere, both in this world and in the next.

Like strangers in an unfamiliar country walking over a hidden treasure, day by day we enter the world of Brahman while in deep sleep but never find it, carried away by what is false.

The Self is hidden in the lotus of the heart. Those who see themselves in all creatures go day by day into the world of Brahman hidden in the heart. Established in peace, they rise above body-consciousness to the supreme light of the Self. Immortal, free from fear, this Self is Brahman, called the True. Beyond the mortal and the immortal, he binds both worlds together. Those who know this live day after day in heaven in this very life.

The Self is a bulwark against the confounding of these worlds and a bridge between them. Day and night cannot cross that bridge, nor old age, nor death, nor grief, nor evil or good deeds. All evils turn back there, unable to cross; evil comes not into this world of Brahman.

One who crosses by this bridge, therefore, if blind, is blind no more; if hurt, ceases to be hurt; if in sorrow, ceases sorrowing. At this boundary night itself becomes day: night comes not into this world of Brahman.

Only those who are pure and self-controlled can find this world of Brahman. That world is theirs alone. In that world, in all the worlds, they live in perfect freedom. ⊸

Finding Unity

Those who know do not speak;
Those who speak do not know.
Stop up the openings,
Close down the doors,
Rub off the sharp edges.
Unravel all confusion.
Harmonize the light,
Give up contention:
This is called finding the unity of life.

When love and hatred cannot affect you,
Profit and loss cannot touch you,
Praise and blame cannot ruffle you,
You are honored by all the world. ↢

I Am the Resurrection & the Life

I am the resurrection and the life, saith the Lord;
He that believeth in me, though he were dead, yet shall he live;
   and whosoever liveth and believeth in me shall never die.

None of us liveth to himself, and no man dieth to himself.
   For if we live, we live unto the Lord,
   and if we die, we die unto the Lord.
Whether we live, therefore, or die, we are the Lord's.

The eternal God is thy refuge, and underneath are the
   everlasting arms.
God is our hope and strength, a very present help in trouble.
Therefore will we not fear, though the earth be moved,
   and though the hills be carried into the midst of the sea;
Though the waters thereof rage and swell,
   and though the mountains shake
   at the tempest of the same.

There is a river, the streams whereof make glad the city of God,
   the holy place of the tabernacle of the Most Highest.
God is in the midst of her, therefore shall she not be removed.

Be still then, and know that I am God.

Lord, thou hast been our refuge
    from one generation to another.
Before the mountains were brought forth,
    or ever the earth and the world were made,
Thou art God from everlasting, and the world without end.
For a thousand years in thy sight are but as yesterday
    when it is past, and as a watch in the night.

Neither death, nor life, nor angels, nor principalities, nor
    powers, nor things present, nor things to come,
    nor height, nor depth, nor any other creature,
shall be able to separate us from the love of God.

Our light affliction, which is but for a moment,
worketh for us a far more exceeding and eternal weight
    of glory;
While we do not look at the things which are seen,
    but at the things which are not seen:
For the things which are seen are temporal,
    but the things which are not seen are eternal.

We know that if our earthly house of this tabernacle
    were dissolved, we have a building of God,
    a house not made with hands, eternal in the heavens. ✎

The Opening

In the name of God, most gracious, most merciful.

Praise be to God, cherisher and sustainer of all.

Most gracious, most merciful,

Thee do we worship, and thine aid we seek.

Show us the straight way, the way of those

on whom thou bestowest grace,

those without wrath, who will not go astray. ⊷

Worship the Lord in Gladness

Raise a shout for the Lord, all the earth;
worship the Lord in gladness;
come into His presence with shouts of joy.
Acknowledge that the Lord is God;
He made us and we are His,
His people, the flock He tends.
Enter His gates with praise,
His courts with acclamation.
Praise Him!
Bless His name!
For the Lord is good;
His steadfast love is eternal;
His faithfulness is for all generations. ❧

United in Heart

May we be united in heart.
May we be united in speech.
May we be united in mind.
May we perform our duties
As did the wise of old.

May we be united in our prayer.
May we be united in our goal.
May we be united in our resolve.
May we be united in our understanding.
May we be united in our offering.
May we be united in our feelings.
May we be united in our hearts.
May we be united in our thoughts.
May there be perfect unity amongst us. ᛫

Prayer for the Peace of the World

O Thou, the Almighty Sun,
    whose light cleareth away all clouds,
    we take refuge in Thee,
    King of men, God of all deities,
    Lord of all angels.
We pray Thee
    dispel the mists of illusion
    from the hearts of the nations
    and lift their lives
    by Thy all-sufficient power.
Pour upon them
    Thy limitless love
    Thy everlasting life
    Thy heavenly joy
    and Thy perfect peace ✧

Adon Olam

The Lord of the universe
Ruled before creation.
When by his will all things came to be,
The name of the Lord was known.
As the Lord creates, he may end the creation,
Remaining alone, unmanifested.
He was, he is, and he shall remain eternal.
He is without beginning;
He is without end.
He is my God, my living strength,
My refuge when I grieve.
He is my only desire.
I live in him alone.
My soul abides in his hands
In sleep as in wakefulness.
Though I leave my body
I will not fear,
For the Lord is with my soul. ✧

Living on Love

On the evening of love, speaking without parable,
Jesus said: "If anyone wishes to love me
All his life, let him keep my Word.
My Father and I will come to visit him.
And we will make his heart our dwelling.
Coming to him, we shall love him always.
We want him to remain, filled with peace,
      In our Love . . ."

Living on Love is holding You Yourself,
Uncreated Word, Word of my God.
Ah! Divine Jesus, you know I love you.
The Spirit of Love sets me aflame with his fire.
In loving you I attract the Father.
My weak heart holds him forever.
O Trinity! You are Prisoner
      Of my Love! . . .

Living on Love is living on your life,
Glorious King, delight of the elect.
You live for me, hidden in a host.
I want to hide myself in you, O Jesus!
Lovers must have solitude,
A heart-to-heart lasting night and day.

Just one glance of yours makes my beatitude.

> I live on Love! . . .

Living on Love is giving without limit
Without claiming any wages here below.
Ah! I give without counting, truly sure
That when one loves, one does not keep count! . . .
Overflowing with tenderness, I have given everything,
To his Divine Heart . . . lightly I run.
I have nothing left but my only wealth:

> Living on Love.

Living on Love is banishing every fear,
Every memory of past faults.
I see no imprint of my sins.
In a moment love has burned everything . . .
Divine Flame, O very sweet Blaze!
I make my home in your hearth.
In your fire I gladly sing:

> "I live on Love! . . ."

Living on Love is keeping within oneself
A great treasure in an earthen vase.
My Beloved, my weakness is extreme.
Ah, I'm far from being an angel from heaven!
But if I fall with each passing hour,
You come to my aid, lifting me up.
At each moment you give me your grace:

> I live on Love.

Living on Love is sailing unceasingly,
Sowing peace and joy in every heart.
Beloved Pilot, Charity impels me,
For I see you in my sister souls.
Charity is my only star.
In its brightness I sail straight ahead.
I've my motto written on my sail:
       "Living on Love."

Living on Love, when Jesus is sleeping,
Is rest on stormy seas.
Oh! Lord, don't fear that I'll wake you.
I'm waiting in peace for Heaven's shore . . .
Faith will soon tear its veil.
My hope is to see you one day.
Charity swells and pushes my sail:
       I live on Love! . . .

Dying of Love is what I hope for.
When I shall see my bonds broken,
My God will be my Great Reward.
I don't desire to possess other goods.
I want to be set on fire with his Love.
I want to see Him, to unite myself to Him forever.
That is my Heaven . . . that is my destiny:
       Living on Love!!! . . . ✛

Mother of All Things

The universe had a beginning
Called the Mother of All Things.
Once you have found the Mother
You can know her children.
Having known the children,
Hold tightly to the Mother.
Your whole life will be preserved from peril.

Open up the openings,
Multiply your affairs,
Your whole life will become a burden.

Those who see the small are called clear-headed;
Those who hold to gentleness are called strong.

Use the light.
Come home to your true nature.
Don't cause yourself injury:
This is known as seizing truth. ✦

The Razor's Edge

In the secret cave of the heart, two are
Seated by life's fountain. The separate ego
Drinks of the sweet and bitter stuff,
Liking the sweet, disliking the bitter,
While the supreme Self drinks sweet and bitter
Neither liking this nor disliking that.
The ego gropes in darkness, while the Self
Lives in light. So declare the illumined sages,
And the householders who worship
The sacred fire in the name of the Lord.

May we light the fire of Nachiketa
That burns out the ego, and enables us
To pass from fearful fragmentation
To fearless fullness in the changeless Whole.

Know the Self as lord of the chariot,
The body as the chariot itself,
The discriminating intellect as
The charioteer, and the mind as the reins.
The senses, say the wise, are the horses;
Selfish desires are the roads they travel.
When the Self is confused with the body,
Mind, and senses, they point out, it seems

To enjoy pleasure and suffer sorrow.
When a person lacks discrimination
And his mind is undisciplined, his senses
Run hither and thither like wild horses.
But they obey the rein like trained horses
When a person has discrimination
And the mind is one-pointed. Those who lack
Discrimination, with little control
Over their thoughts and far from pure,
Reach not the pure state of immortality
But wander from death to death; while those
Who have discrimination, with a still mind
And a pure heart, reach journey's end,
Never again to fall into the jaws of death.
With a discriminating intellect
As charioteer, a well-trained mind as reins,
They attain the supreme goal of life,
To be united with the Lord of Love.

The senses derive from objects of sense-perception,
Sense-objects from mind, mind from intellect,
And intellect from ego; ego from undifferentiated
Consciousness, and consciousness from Brahman.
Brahman is the first Cause and last refuge.
Brahman, the hidden Self in everyone,
Does not shine forth. He is revealed only
To those who keep their minds one-pointed
On the Lord of Love and thus develop

A superconscious manner of knowing.
Meditation empowers them to go
Deeper and deeper into consciousness,
From the world of words to the world of thought,
Then beyond thoughts to wisdom in the Self.

Get up! Wake up! Seek the guidance of an
Illumined teacher and realize the Self.
Sharp like a razor's edge is the path,
The sages say, difficult to traverse.

The supreme Self is beyond name and form,
Beyond the senses, inexhaustible,
Without beginning, without end,
Beyond time, space, and causality, eternal,
Immutable. Those who realize the Self
Are forever free from the jaws of death.

The wise, who gain experiential knowledge
Of this timeless tale of Nachiketa
Narrated by Death, attain the glory
Of living in spiritual awareness.
Those who, full of devotion, recite this
Supreme mystery at a spiritual
Gathering are fit for eternal life.
They are indeed fit for eternal life. ⬦

Entering into Joy

Imagine if all the tumult of the body were to quiet
down, along with all our busy thoughts about earth,
sea, and air; if the very world should stop, and the
mind cease thinking about itself, go beyond itself,
and be quite still;

if all the fantasies that appear in dreams and
imagination should cease, and there be no speech,
no sign:

Imagine if all things that are perishable grew still – for if
we listen they are saying, *We did not make ourselves; he
made us who abides forever* – imagine, then, that they
should say this and fall silent, listening to the very voice
of him who made them and not to that of his creation;

so that we should hear not his word through the
tongues of men, nor the voice of angels, nor the clouds'
thunder, nor any symbol, but the very Self which in
these things we love, and go beyond ourselves to attain
a flash of that eternal wisdom which abides above all
things:

And imagine if that moment were to go on and on, leaving behind all other sights and sounds but this one vision which ravishes and absorbs and fixes the beholder in joy; so that the rest of eternal life were like that moment of illumination which leaves us breathless:

Would this not be what is bidden in scripture,
Enter thou into the joy of thy lord? ✧

Prayer for Peace

Send us Thy peace, O Lord,
    which is perfect and everlasting,
    that our souls may radiate peace.
Send us Thy peace, O Lord,
    that we may think, act, and speak harmoniously.
Send us Thy peace, O Lord,
    that we may be contented and
    thankful for Thy bountiful gifts.
Send us Thy peace, O Lord,
    that amidst our worldly strife
    we may enjoy Thy bliss.
Send us Thy peace, O Lord,
    that we may endure all, tolerate all
    in the thought of Thy grace and mercy.
Send us Thy peace, O Lord,
    that our lives may become a divine vision,
    and in Thy light all darkness may vanish.
Send us Thy peace, O Lord,
    our Father and Mother,
    that we, Thy children on earth,
    may all unite in one family. ✢

Lord, You Are My God

Lord, you are my God.
From dawn I seek you.
My soul thirsts for you,
Like earth dry and parched,
Without water.
I have contemplated you
In the sanctuary,
I have seen your power and glory.
Your love is worth more than life;
Your praise will stay on my lips.

All my life I will bless you;
Lifting my hands, I will call your name.
I will be satisfied as by a feast;
Joyfully I will sing your praise.
In the night I remember you.
I spend hours speaking to you.
Truly you have come to my aid;
I shout for joy in the shadow of your wings.
My soul clings to you;
Your right hand holds me up. ❧

A Garden beyond Paradise

Everything you see has its roots
    in the Unseen world.
The forms may change,
    yet the essence remains the same.

Every wondrous sight will vanish,
Every sweet word will fade.
    But do not be disheartened,
The Source they come from is eternal –
Growing, branching out,
    giving new life and new joy.

Why do you weep? –
That Source is within you,
And this whole world
    is springing up from it.

The Source is full,
Its waters are ever-flowing;
    Do not grieve,
      drink your fill!
Don't think it will ever run dry –
This is the endless Ocean!

From the moment you came into this world
A ladder was placed in front of you
    that you might escape.
From earth you became plant,
From plant you became animal.
Afterwards you became a human being,
Endowed with knowledge, intellect, and faith.

Behold the body, born of dust –
    how perfect it has become!
Why should you fear its end?
When were you ever made less by dying?

When you pass beyond this human form,
No doubt you will become an angel
And soar through the heavens!
But don't stop there.
Even heavenly bodies grow old.

Pass again from the heavenly realm
    and plunge into the vast ocean of Consciousness.
Let the drop of water that is you
    become a hundred mighty seas.

But do not think that the drop alone
Becomes the Ocean –
    the Ocean, too, becomes the drop! ☙

Silence

I weave a silence onto my lips.
I weave a silence into my mind.
I weave a silence within my heart.
I close my ears to distractions.
I close my eyes to attractions.
I close my heart to temptations.

Calm me, O Lord, as you stilled the storm.
Still me, O Lord, keep me from harm.
Let all tumult within me cease.
Enfold me, Lord, in your peace. ✧

The Shining Essence

I look into the mirror and see my own beauty;
I see the truth of the universe revealing itself as me.

I rise in the sky as the morning Sun, do not be surprised,
Every particle of creation is me alone.

What are the holy spirits? my essence revealed.
And the human body? the vessel of my own form.

What is the ocean that encircles the world?
A drop of my abundant Grace;
And the purest light that fills every soul?
A spark of my own illumination.

I am Light itself, reflected in the heart of everyone;
I am the treasure of the Divine Name,
    the shining Essence of all things.

I am every light that shines,
Every ray that illumines the world.
From the highest heavens to the bedrock of the earth
All is but a shadow of my splendor.

If I dropped the veil covering my true essence
The world would be gone – lost in a brilliant light.

What is the water that gives eternal life?
A drop of my divine nectar.
And the breath that brings the dead back to life?
A puff of my breath, the breath of all life. ↤

The Earth Is the Lord's

The earth is the Lord's, and the fullness thereof;
    the world, and they that dwell therein.
For He hath founded it upon the seas,
    and established it upon the floods.
Who shall ascend into the mountain of the Lord?
    And who shall stand in His holy place?
He that hath clean hands, and a pure heart;
    who hath not taken His name in vain,
    and hath not sworn deceitfully.
He shall receive a blessing from the Lord,
    and righteousness from the God of his salvation.
Such is the generation of them that seek after Him,
    that seek Thy face, even Jacob.
Lift up your heads, O ye gates,
    and be ye lifted up, ye everlasting doors;
    that the King of glory may come in.
Who is the King of glory? The Lord strong and mighty,
    the Lord mighty in battle.
Lift up your heads, O ye gates,
    yea, lift them up,
    ye everlasting doors;
    that the King of glory may come in.
Who then is the King of glory?
    The Lord of hosts; He is the King of glory. ✎

Be Aware of Me Always

SRI KRISHNA

Those who are free from selfish attachments,
Who have mastered the senses and passions,
Act not, but are acted through by the Lord.
Listen to me now, O son of Kunti,
How one who has become an instrument
In the hands of the Lord attains Brahman,
The supreme consummation of wisdom.

Unerring in discrimination,
Sovereign of the senses and passions,
Free from the clamor of likes and dislikes,
They lead a simple, self-reliant life
Based on meditation, using speech,
Body, and mind to serve the Lord of Love.

Free from self-will, aggressiveness, arrogance,
From the lust to possess people or things,
They are at peace with themselves and others
And enter into the unitive state.

United with the Lord, ever joyful,
Beyond the reach of self-will and sorrow,
They serve me in every living creature

And attain supreme devotion to me.
By loving me they share in my glory
And enter into my boundless being.
All their acts are performed in my service,
And through my grace they win eternal life.

Make every act an offering to me;
Regard me as your only protector.
Make every thought an offering to me;
Meditate on me always.

Drawing upon your deepest resources,
You shall overcome all difficulties
Through my grace. But if you will not heed me
In your self-will, nothing will avail you.

If you say, "I will not fight this battle,"
Your own nature will drive you into it.
If you will not fight the battle of life,
Your own karma will drive you into it.

The Lord dwells in the hearts of all creatures,
And he whirls them round on the wheel of time.
Run to him for refuge with all your strength
And peace profound will be yours through his grace.

I give you these precious words of wisdom;
Reflect on them and then choose what is best.
These are the last words I shall speak to you,
Dear one, for your spiritual fulfillment.

Be aware of me always, adore me,
Make every act an offering to me,
And you shall come to me;
This I promise, for you are dear to me.
Leave all other support, and look to me
For protection. I shall purify you
From the sins of the past. Do not grieve.

Do not share this wisdom with anyone
Who lacks in devotion or self-control,
Lacks the desire to learn, or who scoffs at me.

Those who teach this supreme mystery
Of the Gita to all those who love me
Will come to me without doubt. No one
Can render me more devoted service;
No one on earth can be more dear to me.

Those who meditate on these holy words
Worship me with wisdom and devotion.
Even those who listen to them with faith,
Free from doubts, will find a happier world.

Have you fully understood my message?
Are you free from your doubts and delusions?

ARJUNA

You have dispelled my doubts and delusions
And made me ready to fight this battle.
My faith is firm now, and I will do your will. ❧

The Sermon on the Mount

Ye have heard that it hath been said,
Thou shalt love thy neighbor, and hate thine enemy.
But I say unto you,

Love your enemies, bless them that curse you,
do good to them that hate you, and pray for them
which despitefully use you, and persecute you;
that ye may be the children of your Father which is in
heaven: for he maketh his sun to rise on the evil and on the
good, and sendeth rain on the just and on the unjust.

For if ye love them which love you, what reward have ye?
Do not even the publicans the same? And if ye salute your
brethren only, what do ye more than others?
Do not even the publicans so?

Be ye therefore perfect,
even as your Father which is in heaven is perfect. ✦

Remembrance of God

Those who are content, needing nothing,
and seek solitude in meditation will find peace.

Those who have trodden all selfish desires underfoot
will find freedom.

Those who have rid themselves of envy will find friendship.

Those who have patience, even for a little while,
will find themselves prepared for Eternity.

God has said: "When my servant becomes altogether
occupied with me, repeating my Name, then I make his
happiness consist in remembrance of me. And when I have
made his happiness consist in the remembrance of me, he
desires me and I desire him. And when he desires me and I
desire him, I raise the veils between me and him and reveal
myself before his eyes." ↔

Believing in Mind

The great Way has no impediments;
It does not pick and choose.
When you abandon attachment and aversion
You see it plainly.
Make a thousandth of an inch distinction,
Heaven and earth swing apart.
If you want it to appear before your eyes,
Cherish neither *for* nor *against*.

To compare what you like with what you dislike,
That is the disease of the mind.
You pass over the hidden meaning;
Peace of mind is needlessly troubled.

It is round and perfect like vast space,
Lacks nothing, never overflows.
Only because we take and reject
Do we lose the means to know its Suchness.

Don't get tangled in outward desire
Or get caught within yourself.
Once you plant deep the longing for peace
Confusion leaves of itself.

Return to the root and find meaning;
Follow sense objects, you lose the goal.
Just one instant of inner enlightenment
Will take you far beyond the emptiness of the world.

Selfish attachment forgets all limits;
It always leads down evil roads.
When you let go of it, things happen of themselves;
The substance neither goes nor abides.

If the eye does not sleep
All dreams will naturally stop.
If the mind does not differentiate
All things are of one Suchness.

When you fathom the realm of Suchness
You instantly forget all selfish desire.
Having seen ten thousand things as one
You return to your natural state.

Without meditation
Consciousness and feeling are hard to grasp.
In the realm of Suchness
There is neither self nor other.

In the one, there is the all.
In the all, there is the one.
If you know this,
You will never worry about being incomplete.

If belief and mind are made the same
And there is no division between belief and mind
The road of words comes to an end,
Beyond present and future. ⊷

Duties of the Heart

What is meant by wholehearted devotion to God alone?

It means that in every act, public and private, the aim and purpose should be purely work for God's sake, to please him only, without winning the approval of other people.

How achieve wholehearted devotion to God alone? In ten ways. If these are firmly set in your heart and you clearly make them the basis of your actions, then your devotion to God will be complete. Then you will turn to no one else, set your hope on nothing else, and mold your will to none other than God's.

First is wholehearted acceptance that only God fills the universe;

Second, that God is the source of all reality and is endlessly good;

Third, that your goal is to work for God;

Fourth, that you should rely on God alone and
not on physical beings;

Fifth, that you get no ultimate gain or loss
from physical beings, but only from the Creator;

Sixth, that you should maintain evenness of mind
regardless of whether people praise you or blame
you;

Seventh, that you should not make a show of
spiritual activities to impress other people;

Eighth, that you should not be caught up in personal
gain when you are working for eternal life;

Ninth, that you should hold God in reverence and
be humble before him;

Tenth, that you should use your mind to master your
senses and use them with care and discrimination. ✦

When You Call

Then, when you call, the Lord will answer;
When you cry, He will say: *Here I am.*
If you banish the yoke from your midst,
The menacing hand and evil speech,
And you offer your compassion to the hungry
And satisfy the famished creature –
Then shall your light shine in darkness,
And your gloom shall be like noonday.
The Lord will guide you always;
He will slake your thirst in parched places
And give strength to your bones.
You shall be like a watered garden,
Like a spring whose waters do not fail. ❧

The One Appearing as Many

May the Lord of Love, who projects himself
Into the universe of myriad forms
Through maya, from whom all beings come,
To whom all beings finally return,
May he grant us the grace of wisdom.

He is the fire and the sun, and the moon
And the stars. He is the air and the sea,
And the creator Prajapati.

He is this boy, he is that girl; he is
This man, he is that woman, and he is
This old man, too, tottering on his staff.
His face is seen everywhere.

He is the blue bird, he is the green bird
With red eyes; he is the thundercloud, and
He is the seasons and the seas; he has
No beginning, he has no end. He is
The source from whom all the worlds evolve.

From his divine power of maya comes
Forth this magical show of name and form,

Of you and me, which casts the spell of pain
And pleasure. When we pierce through the magic,
We see the One who appears as many.

Two birds of beautiful plumage, comrades
Inseparable, live on the same tree.
One bird eats the fruit of pleasure and pain;
The other looks on without eating.

Forgetting our divine origin, we
Become ensnared in the world of maya
And bewail our helplessness. But when we
See the Lord of Love in all his glory,
Adored by all, we go beyond sorrow.

What use are the scriptures to anyone
Who knows not the one source from whom they come,
In whom all gods and worlds abide? Only
They who realize him as ever present
In their hearts attain abiding joy.

The Lord, who is the supreme magician,
Brings forth out of himself all the scriptures,
Oblations, sacrifices, spiritual
Disciplines, past and present, and the whole
Universe. Though he is not visible,
He remains hidden in the hearts of all.

Know him to be the supreme magician
Who has brought all the worlds out of himself.
Know that all beings in the universe
Partake of his divine splendor.

Know him to be the supreme magician
Who has become boy and girl, bird and beast.
He is the bestower of all blessings,
And his grace fills the heart with peace profound.
Know him to be the supreme source of all
The gods, support of the universe,
And sower of the golden seed of life.
May he grant us the grace of wisdom.

Know him to be the supreme God of gods,
From whom all the worlds draw their breath of life.
He rules every creature from within.
May he be worshipped by everyone.

Know him to be the supreme pervader,
In whom the whole universe is smaller
Than the smallest atom. May he, Shiva,
Fill our heart with infinite peace.

Know him to be the supreme guardian
Of the cosmos, protecting all creatures
From within. May he, Shiva, in whom all
Are one, free us from the bonds of death.

Know him to be the Supreme One, hidden
In the hearts of all as cream is in milk
And yet encompassing the universe.
May he, Shiva, free us from all bondage.

Know him to be the supreme architect
Who is enshrined in the hearts of all.
Know him in the depths of meditation.
May he grant us immortality.

Know him to be the supreme source of all
Religions, ruler of the world of light,
Where there is neither day nor night, neither
What is nor what is not, but only Shiva.
He is beyond the reach of the mind.
He alone is. His glory fills all worlds.

He is beyond the reach of the eye.
He alone is. May he, Shiva, reveal
Himself in the depths of meditation
And grant us immortality.

I live in fear of death, O Lord of Love;
I seek refuge at your feet. Protect me,
Protect us, man and woman, cow and horse.
May the brave ones who seek you be released
From the bondage of death. ⟿

JUDAH HALEVY ⟿

Lord, Where Shall I Find You?

Lord, where shall I find you?
Your place is lofty and secret.
And where shall I not find you?
The whole earth is full of your glory!
You are found in our innermost heart,
yet you fixed earth's boundaries.
You are a strong tower for those who are near
and the trust of those who go far.
I have sought to come near you;
I have called to you with all my heart;
and when I went out towards you,
I found you coming towards me. ⟿

Invocation

May the Lord of day grant us peace.

May the Lord of night grant us peace.

May the Lord of sight grant us peace.

May the Lord of might grant us peace.

May the Lord of speech grant us peace.

May the Lord of space grant us peace.

I bow down to Brahman, source of all power.

I will speak the truth and follow the law.

Guard me and my teacher against all harm.

Guard me and my teacher against all harm.

This Morning I Pray

This morning, as I kindle the fire on my hearth,
    I pray that the flame of God's love may burn in
    my heart and in the hearts of all I meet today.

I pray that no envy or malice,
    no hatred or fear, may smother the flame.

I pray that indifference and apathy, contempt and pride,
    may not pour like cold water on the fire.

Instead, may the spark of God's love
    light the love in my heart,
    that it may burn brightly through the day.

And may I warm those who are lonely,
    whose hearts are cold and lifeless,
    so that all may know the comfort of God's love. ✤

The Immortal

There is a city with eleven gates
Of which the ruler is the unborn Self,
Whose light forever shines.
They go beyond sorrow who meditate on the Self
And are freed from the cycle of birth and death.
For this Self is supreme!

The Self is the sun shining in the sky,
The wind blowing in space; he is the fire
At the altar and in the home the guest;
He dwells in human beings, in gods, in truth,
And in the vast firmament; he is the fish
Born in water, the plant growing in the earth,
The river flowing down from the mountain.
For this Self is supreme!

The adorable one who is seated
In the heart rules the breath of life.
Unto him all the senses pay their homage.
When the dweller in the body breaks out
In freedom from the bonds of flesh, what remains?
For this Self is supreme!

We live not by the breath that flows in
And flows out, but by him who causes the breath
To flow in and flow out.

Now, O Nachiketa, I will tell you
Of this unseen, eternal Brahman, and
What befalls the Self after death.
Of those unaware of the Self, some are born
As embodied creatures while others remain
In a lower stage of evolution,
As determined by their own need for growth.

That which is awake even in our sleep,
Giving form in dreams to the objects of
Sense craving, that indeed is pure light,
Brahman the immortal, who contains all
The cosmos, and beyond whom none can go.
For this Self is supreme!

As the same fire assumes different shapes
When it consumes objects differing in shape,
So does the one Self take the shape
Of every creature in whom he is present.
As the same air assumes different shapes
When it enters objects differing in shape,
So does the one Self take the shape
Of every creature in whom he is present.

As the sun, who is the eye of the world,
Cannot be tainted by the defects in our eyes
Or by the objects it looks on,
So the one Self, dwelling in all, cannot
Be tainted by the evils of the world.
For this Self transcends all!

The ruler supreme, inner Self of all,
Multiplies his oneness into many.
Eternal joy is theirs who see the Self
In their own hearts. To none else does it come!
Changeless amidst the things that pass away,
Pure consciousness in all who are conscious,
The One answers the prayers of many.
Eternal peace is theirs who see the Self
In their own hearts. To none else does it come!

NACHIKETA

How can I know that blissful Self, supreme,
Inexpressible, realized by the wise?
Is he the light, or does he reflect light?

THE KING OF DEATH

There shines not the sun, neither moon nor star,
Nor flash of lightning, nor fire lit on earth.
The Self is the light reflected by all.
He shining, everything shines after him. ✧

The Temple of the Lord

As oil is in the oil seed,
And fire is in the flint,
So is the Lord within thee, unrevealed.
Follow thy Master's simple and true instructions,
Keep vigil strict at midnight and so find Him.

As fragrance is within the flower's blossom,
So is the Lord within thee, unrevealed.
But as the musk-deer searches for musk in forest grass,
So does man search for Him outside
And finds Him not.

As the pupil is within the eye itself,
So is the Lord within thy body;
But fools know not this simple fact,
And search for Him elsewhere.

As air pervades all space,
But none can see it,
So does the Lord pervade the body;
But He remains to each one unrevealed,
Since the lodestone of the heart is not attached to Him.
O man, the object of supremest value,

For which you search throughout the world,
    is here within you,
But the veil of Illusion ever separates you from Him.
Tear the veil boldly asunder and you will find Him.

My Lord is living in each human being;
There is no bridal bed without the Bridegroom.
But blessed is the body
In which He reveals Himself.

As fragrance is in the flower,
So is the Lord within thee.
But He reveals Himself in His beloved Saints;
That is all you need to know. Go forth and meet them. ❧

Remember Me through Grace

The Lord says:
Remember me through grace;
I will remember you through mercy.
Remember Me in prayer;
I will remember you in giving.
Remember Me in this world;
I will remember you in the next.
Remember Me in solitude;
I will remember you openly.
Remember Me with repentance;
I will remember you with forgiveness. ✤

Dwell, O Mind, Within Yourself

Dwell, O mind, within yourself;
Enter no other's home.
If you but seek there, you will find
All you are searching for.

God, the true Philosopher's Stone,
Who answers every prayer,
Lies hidden deep within your heart,
The richest gem of all.

How many pearls and precious stones
Are scattered all about
The outer court that lies before
The chamber of your heart! ⟿

The Mirror of Eternity

Place your mind before the mirror of eternity,
place your soul in the brightness of His glory,
place your heart in the image of the divine essence
and transform yourself by contemplation
    utterly into the image of His divinity,
that you too may feel what His friends feel as they taste
    the hidden sweetness that God himself has set aside
    from the beginning for those who love Him.

Casting aside all things in this false and troubled world
    that ensnare those who love them blindly,
    give all your love to Him who gave Himself in all
    for you to love:
Whose beauty the sun and moon admire, and whose gifts
    are abundant and precious and grand without end. ↩

I Come to Him Running

The Prophet said,

God Most High has said:
When my worshipper's thoughts turn to Me,
there am I with him.
And when he makes mention of Me within himself,
I make mention of him within Myself:
and when he makes mention of Me in company,
I make mention of him in a better company.
If he draw near to Me a hand's breadth,
I draw near to him an arm's length;
and if he draw near to Me an arm's length,
I draw near to him the length of both arms
wide outstretched;
and if he come to Me walking, I come to him running.
And if he meet Me with sins equivalent to the whole world,
I will greet him with forgiveness equal to it. ❧

The Saint

They have completed their voyage; they have gone beyond
sorrow. The fetters of life have fallen from them, and they
live in full freedom.

The thoughtful strive always. They have no fixed abode,
but leave home like swans from their lake.

Like the flight of birds in the sky, the path of the selfless
is hard to follow. They have no possessions, but live on
alms in a world of freedom. Like the flight of birds in the
sky, their path is hard to follow. With their senses under
control, temperate in eating, they know the meaning of
freedom.

Even the gods envy the saints, whose senses obey them
like well-trained horses and who are free from pride.
Patient like the earth, they stand like a threshold. They are
pure like a lake without mud, and free from the cycle of
birth and death.

Wisdom has stilled their minds, and their thoughts,
words, and deeds are filled with peace. Freed from illusion

and from personal ties, they have renounced the world of appearance to find reality. Thus have they reached the highest.

They make holy wherever they dwell, in village or forest, on land or at sea. With their senses at peace and minds full of joy, they make the forests holy. ✦

Come, Beloved

As the lotus dies without water,
As the night is blind without the moon,
So is my heart without you, Beloved.
I wander alone at night,
Driven by my longing for you.
I hunger for you all the day,
I thirst for you all the night.

My grief is beyond words;
My mind is beyond rest.
Come and end my grief, Beloved.
Come and bring joy to my heart.
You know my inmost secret;
Then look at me with eyes of love,
Your slave for countless lives
        since the dawn of time.
So says Meera at your feet. ✧

The Path to Your Dwelling

How am I to come to you
When I stand outside a locked gate?
The path to your dwelling
Runs steep and dangerous.
In fear I climb, step by step,
The path to your dwelling,
So steep and dangerous.
O Lord, you seem so far away
That my mind goes up and down.
As I climb, the sentinels watch
And the robbers wait to waylay me.
Though the path to your dwelling
Is steep and dangerous,
You have called me home.
Meera's wanderings are ended.
She has found her way to your feet. ✧

Life of My Life

You are the life of my life,
 O Krishna, the heart of my heart.
There is none in all the three worlds
Whom I call my own but you.

You are the peace of my mind;
You are the joy of my heart;
You are my beauty and my wealth.

You are my wisdom and my strength;
I call you my home, my friend, my kin.

My present and future are in your hands;
My scriptures and commands come from you.
Supreme teacher, fountain of wisdom,
You are the path and the goal,
Tender mother and stern father too.

You are the creator and protector,
And the pilot who takes me across
The stormy ocean of life. ✣

Let Me Walk in Beauty

O Great Spirit,
    whose voice I hear in the winds
    and whose breath gives life to all the world,
    hear me.
I am small and weak.
I need your strength and wisdom.

Let me walk in beauty
    and let my eyes ever behold the red and purple sunset.
Make my hands respect the things you have made
    and my ears grow sharp to hear your voice.

Make me wise so that I may understand the things
    you have taught my people.
Let me learn the lessons you have hidden
    in every leaf and rock.
I seek strength not to be greater than my brother or sister
    but to fight my greatest enemy, myself.
Make me always ready
    to come to you with clean hands and straight eyes
So when life fades as the fading sunset
    my spirit may come to you without shame. ↔

Her Heart Is Full of Joy

Her heart is full of joy with love,
For in the Lord her mind is stilled.
She has renounced every selfish attachment
And draws abiding joy and strength
From the One within.
She lives not for herself, but lives
To serve the Lord of Love in all,
And swims across the sea of life
Breasting its rough waves joyfully. ✣

The Tree of Eternity

The Tree of Eternity has its roots above
And its branches on earth below.
Its pure root is Brahman the immortal,
From whom all the worlds draw their life, and whom
None can transcend. For this Self is supreme!

The cosmos comes forth from Brahman and moves
In him. With his power it reverberates,
Like thunder crashing in the sky. Those who realize him
Pass beyond the sway of death.

In fear of him fire burns; in fear of him
The sun shines, the clouds rain, and the winds blow.
In fear of him death stalks about to kill.

If one fails to realize Brahman in this life
Before the physical sheath is shed,
He must again put on a body
In the world of embodied creatures.

Brahman can be seen, as in a mirror,
In a pure heart; in the world of the ancestors
As in a dream; in the gandharva world

As the reflections in trembling waters;
And clear as light in the realm of the Creator.
Knowing the senses to be separate
From the Self, and the sense experience
To be fleeting, the wise grieve no more.

Above the senses is the mind,
Above the mind is the intellect, above that
Is the ego, and above the ego
Is the unmanifested Cause.
And beyond is Brahman, omnipresent,
Attributeless. Realizing him one is released
From the cycle of birth and death.

He is formless, and can never be seen
With these two eyes. But he reveals himself
In the heart made pure through meditation
And sense-restraint. Realizing him one is released
From the cycle of birth and death.

When the five senses are stilled, when the mind
Is stilled, when the intellect is stilled,
That is called the highest state by the wise.
They say yoga is this complete stillness
In which one enters the unitive state,
Never to become separate again.
If one is not established in this state,
The sense of unity will come and go.

The unitive state cannot be attained
Through words or thoughts or through the eye.
How can it be attained except through one who is
Established in this state himself?
There are two selves, the separate ego
And the indivisible Atman.
When one rises above I, me, and mine,
The Atman is revealed as one's real Self.

When all desires that surge in the heart
Are renounced, the mortal becomes immortal.
When all the knots that strangle the heart
Are loosened, the mortal becomes immortal.
This sums up the teaching of the scriptures.

From the heart there radiate a hundred
And one vital tracks. One of them rises
To the crown of the head. This way leads
To immortality, the others to death.

The Lord of Love, not larger than the thumb,
Is ever enshrined in the hearts of all.
Draw him clear out of the physical sheath,
As one draws the stalk from the munja grass.
Know thyself to be pure and immortal!
Know thyself to be pure and immortal! ⇔

The Island

For those struggling in midstream,
 in great fear of the flood,
 of growing old and of dying –
for all those I say, an island exists
 where there is no place for impediments,
 no place for clinging:
the island of no going beyond.

I call it nirvana,
 the complete destruction
 of old age and dying. ❧

All Paths Lead to Me

He who knows me as his own divine Self,
As the operator in him, breaks through
The belief he is the body, and is
Not born separate again. Such a one
Is united with me, O Arjuna.

Delivered from selfish attachment, fear,
And anger, filled with me, surrendering
Themselves to me, purified in the fire
Of my being, many have reached the
State of unity in me.

As people approach me, so I receive them.
All paths lead to me. ❧

The Shema

Hear, O Israel,
 the Lord our God, the Lord is one.
Blessed is his Name,
 whose glorious kingdom is forever.

And you shall love the Lord with all your heart,
and with all your soul, and with all your might.

And these words, which I command you this day,
shall be upon your heart: and you shall teach them
always to your children, and shall talk of them
when you sit in your house, when you walk by the
way, when you lie down, and when you arise.

And you shall bind them as a sign on your hand,
and they will be seen as a badge between your eyes.

And you shall write them on the doorposts of your
house, and upon your gates. ᴼᴾ

If You Want to Draw Near to God

If you want to draw near to God,
seek him in the hearts of those around you.
Speak well of all, present or absent.
If you would be a light for others,
be like the sun: show the same face to all.
To bring joy to a single heart is better
than building countless shrines for worship;
to capture one heart through kindness is better
than setting a thousand free.
This is the true lover of God,
who lives with others,
rises and eats and sleeps like others,
gives and takes with others in the bazaar,
yet never forgets God even for a moment. ⊹

Lord, I Bring Thee My Treasure

Lord, I bring Thee my treasure!
It is greater than the mountains,
Wider than the world,
Deeper than the sea,
Higher than the clouds,
More glorious than the sun,
More manifold than the stars;
It outweighs the whole earth.

O thou image of my divine Godhead,
Ennobled by my humanity,
Adorned by my Holy Spirit,
What is thy treasure called?

Lord, it is called my heart's desire.
I have withdrawn it from the world
And denied it to myself and all creatures.
Now I can bear it no longer.
Where, O Lord, shall I lay it?

Thy heart's desire shalt thou lay nowhere
But in mine own divine heart
And on my human breast.
There alone wilt thou find comfort
And be embraced by my Holy Spirit. ❧

Simple Union

O seeker, the simple union is the best.

Since the day when I met with my Lord,

There has been no end to the sport of our love.

I shut not my eyes, I close not my ears,

I do not mortify my body; I see with eyes open

And smile and behold his beauty everywhere:

I utter his name, and whatever I see,

It reminds me of him; whatever I do,

It becomes his worship.

The rising and the setting are one to me:

All contradictions are solved.

Wherever I go, I move round him.

All I achieve is his service: when I lie down,

I lie prostrate at his feet.

He is the only adorable one to me:

I have none other.

My tongue has left off impure words;

It sings his glory, day and night.

Whether I rise or sit down, I can never forget him,

For the rhythm of his music beats in my ears.

Kabir says: My heart is frenzied

And I disclose in my soul what is hidden.

I am immersed in that great bliss

Which transcends all pleasure and pain. ⊷

Think on His Name

Whilst thou art busy at work,
Think on His name:

Then shall evil be vanquished,
And grief shall be turned into peace:

To this at the end thou must come,
When thy last breath faileth,
And home, children, wealth, are forgotten:

For long thou canst put Him off,
Thou canst live thy life as thou wilt,
But at last thy barque shall be sucked
    to the whirlpool:

Break the snares from thee now,
Do now what thou some day must do:

At the end thou hast one defense,
One only,
Trust in His name.
By this alone thou canst find salvation,
But by this alone:
Then trust in Him now. ↝

Evening Prayer for the Sabbath

In this moment of silent communion with Thee,
   O Lord, a still small voice speaks in the depth
   of my spirit.
It speaks to me of the things I must do to attain
   holy kinship with Thee and to grow
   in the likeness of Thee.
I must do my allotted task with unflagging faithfulness
   even though the eye of no taskmaster is on me.
I must be gentle in the face of ingratitude
   or when slander distorts my noblest motives.
I must come to the end of each day with a feeling
   that I have used its gifts gratefully
   and faced its trials bravely.
O Lord, help me to be ever more like Thee,
   holy for Thou art holy,
   loving for Thou art love.
Speak to me, then, Lord, as I seek Thee again and again
   in the stillness of meditation, until Thy bidding
   shall at last become for me a hallowed discipline,
   a familiar way of life. ✧

The River of Love

I am a citizen of that kingdom
Where reigns the Lord in all His glory;
Neither pain nor pleasure cast their shadows
Where the sun of joy never sets.

I am a citizen of that kingdom
Where every day is a day of celebration;
The river of love overflows its banks,
And the lotus blooms in the devotee's heart.

I am a citizen of that kingdom
Where shines the Lord as the source of light,
And lights the lamp of wisdom in my heart
To burn without oil, without wick. ✦

Four Things That Bring Much Inward Peace

My child, now will I teach thee the way of peace and true liberty.

O Lord, I beseech thee, do as thou sayest, for this is delightful for me to hear.

Be desirous, my child, to work for the welfare of another rather than seek thine own will.
Choose always to have less rather than more.
Seek always the lowest place, and to be inferior to everyone.
Wish always, and pray, that the will of God may be wholly fulfilled in thee.

Behold, such a one entereth within the borders of peace and rest.

O Lord, this short discourse of thine containeth within itself much perfection. It is little to be spoken, but full of meaning, and abundant in fruit. . . . Thou who canst do all things, and ever lovest the profiting of my soul, increase in me thy grace, that I may be able to fulfill thy words, and to work out mine own salvation. ✢

There Is But One God

There is but one God.
Truth is his name,
Maker of all things,
Free from fear and hate,
Timeless, birthless, self-existent,
Known by the grace of the Guru.
Meditate on the True Name,
True in the beginning,
True in all ages.
He is true now
And he shall ever be true, says Nanak. ↬

I Gave All My Heart

I gave all my heart to the Lord of Love,
And my life is so completely transformed
That my Beloved One has become mine
And without a doubt I am his at last.

When that tender hunter from paradise
Released his piercing arrow at me,
My wounded soul fell in his loving arms;
And my life is so completely transformed
That my Beloved One has become mine
And without a doubt I am his at last.

He pierced my heart with his arrow of love
And made me one with the Lord who made me.
This is the only love I have to prove,
And my life is so completely transformed
That my Beloved One has become mine
And without a doubt I am his at last. ❧

Night Prayer

My God and my Lord,
    eyes are at rest,
    stars are setting,
    hushed are the movements of birds
      in their nests,
    of monsters in the deep.
And Thou art the Just who knowest no change,
    the Equity that swerveth not,
    the Everlasting that passeth not away.

The doors of kings are locked,
    watched by their bodyguards;
    but Thy door is open to him who calls on Thee.
My Lord, each lover is now alone with his beloved,
    and Thou art for me the Beloved. ⊷

God Makes the Rivers to Flow

God makes the rivers to flow. They tire not,
    nor do they cease from flowing.
May the river of my life flow into the sea of love
    that is the Lord.

May I overcome all the impediments in my course.
May the thread of my song be not cut before my life
    merges in the sea of love.

Guard me against all danger, O Lord.
Accept megraciously, O King of kings.

Release me from my sorrows, which hold me as ropes
    hold a calf. I cannot even open my eyes without
    the power of your love.

Guard us against the grief that haunts the life of the
    selfish. Lead us from darkness into light.

We will sing of your love as it was sung of old.
Your laws change not, but stand like the mountains.
Forgive me all the mistakes I have committed.
Many mornings will dawn upon us again.
Guide us through them all, O Lord of Love. ✢

That Wondrous Star

She is truly like a star,

That noble star of Jacob
    whose rays illumine the universe,
    shine in the highest heaven,
    penetrate the darkest depths,
    and spread throughout the earth,
    warming goodness like springtime,
    burning out evil.

She is that bright and wondrous star
    forever raised above the great wide sea
    of this world, sparkling with merit,
    a shining guide.

O voyager, whoever you may be,
    when you find yourself in stormy seas
    in danger of foundering in the tempests
    and far from land, lest you sink and drown,
    fix your eyes on this bright star; call out to Mary.

When temptations blow
>or the shoals of tribulation threaten,
>>fix your eyes on this star; call out to Mary.

When the waves of pride or ambition batter your soul,
>of slander or jealousy, anger or lust,
>>fix your eyes on this star; call out to Mary.

In doubt, in danger, in precarious straits,
>fix your mind on Mary; call out to Mary.
Never let her leave you, keep her with you always,
>"even in thy mouth and in thy heart."
Never abandon her presence, never leave her company,
>to win approval in her prayers.

Follow her and you will never lose your way.
Appeal to her and you will never lose hope.
Think of her always and you will never stray.
With her holding you, you cannot fall.
With her protection, you cannot fear.
When she leads, you cannot tire.
With her grace you will come safely
>through to journey's end.
Then you will know for yourself
>why she bears the name Star of the Sea. ✎

Singing Your Name

Singing your name day and night,
It echoes in my mind all the time.
O Krishna, I am the dust of your feet;
How can I lift my voice in your praise?

Singing your name heals all wounds,
And guards the mind against selfish thoughts.

I am armed with the arrow of your name
Fixed on the bow-string of my heart;
I wear the armor of your glory
As I sing of your life and divine deeds.

My body is a musical instrument
On which my mind plays songs of love.

To awaken my soul from sleep,
I sing and dance before the Lord
Waiting for the door to open. ✧

Mourner's Kaddish

May His great Name grow exalted and sanctified
in the world that He created as He willed.
May He give reign to His kingship in your lifetimes
and in your days,
and in the lifetimes of the entire Family of Israel,
swiftly and soon.
May His great Name be blessed forever and ever.
Blessed, praised, glorified, exalted, extolled,
mighty, upraised, and lauded be the Name
of the Holy One,
Blessed is He beyond any blessing and song,
praise, and consolation that are uttered in the world.
May there be abundant peace from Heaven, and life
upon us and upon all Israel.
He Who makes peace in the heights, may He make peace
upon us and upon all Israel. ✛

Weaving Your Name

I weave your name on the loom of my mind
To make my garment when you come to me.
My loom has ten thousand threads
To make my garment when you come to me.
The sun and moon watch while I weave your name;
The sun and moon hear while I count your name.
These are the wages I get by day and night
To deposit in the lotus bank of my heart.

I weave your name on the loom of my mind
To clean and soften ten thousand threads
And to comb the twists and knots of my thoughts.
No more shall I weave a garment of pain.
For you have come to me, drawn by my weaving –
My ceaselessly weaving your name
        on the loom of my mind. ✧

The Fruit of the Tree

No longer am I
The man I used to be;
For I have plucked the fruit
Of this precious tree of life.

As the river flows down the hills
And becomes one with the sea,
So has this weaver's love flowed
To become one with the Lord of Love.

Go deeper and deeper in meditation
To reach the seabed of consciousness.
Through the blessing of my teacher
I have passed beyond the land of death.

Says Kabir: Listen to me, friends,
And cast away all your doubts.
Make your faith unshakable in the Lord,
And pass beyond the land of death. ᛞ

Grieve Not

Grieve Not is the name of my town.
Pain and fear cannot enter there,
Free from possessions, free from life's taxes,
Free from fear of disease and death.

After much wandering I am come back home
Where turns not the wheel of time and change,
And my Emperor rules, without a second or third,
In Abadan, filled with love and wisdom.

The citizens are rich in the wealth of the heart,
And they live ever free in the City of God.
Listen to Ravidas, just a cobbler:
"All who live here are my true friends." ✎

Glossary of Names & Terms

abadan   [Arabic] Forever, eternal, to the end of time.

Abu Sa'id   (967–1049) Persian poet and Sufi mystic.

Ansari of Herat   (1006–1088) Persian poet and Sufi mystic.

Araqi, Fakhruddin   (1213–1289) Persian-born poet and Sufi mystic.

Arjuna   In the Bhagavad Gita, the friend and disciple of Sri Krishna.

Atman   [Sanskrit] The Self; the divine essence in every creature.

Augustine, St.   (354–430) Catholic saint and theologian, one of the most important figures in the development of Western Christianity.

Azikri, Rabbi Eleazar   (1533–1600) Scholar and student of the Kabbalah, a mystical tradition of Judaism.

Baba Kuhi of Shiraz   (d. 1050) Revered Persian Sufi master.

Bahya ibn Pakuda, Rabbi   Eleventh-century Jewish philosopher and mystic in Muslim Spain.

Bernard of Clairvaux, St.   (1090–1153) French Catholic saint and mystic; leader of the Cistercian reform.

Bhagavad Gita   "Song of the Lord," India's best-known scripture.

bodhi   Buddhist term for enlightenment; *nirvana* (lit. "awakening").

Book of Common Prayer   Prayers from the Anglican Christian liturgy.

Brahman   (Hindu) The attributeless Godhead.

brahmin   Priestly caste in Hinduism; more generally, one worthy of realizing Brahman (God).

Buddha   ("Awakened"; b. Siddhartha Gautama, c. 563–483 BC) World teacher who combined intellectual insight with immense compassion.

Catherine of Genoa, St.   (1447–1510) Catholic saint and mystic known for depth of insight and dedicated, compassionate service.

Chandogya Upanishad   One of the oldest of the Upanishads.

Clare of Assisi, St.   (1194–1253) Catholic saint, one of the first followers of St. Francis of Assisi and founder of the Franciscan order for women.

Dhammapada   Ancient popular collection of the Buddha's teachings in verse form.

dharma   [Sanskrit] Truth, righteousness, the central law that all of life is one.

Dov Baer of Mezhirech   (d. 1772) Direct successor of Rabbi Israel ben Eliezar, the "Baal Shem Tov," founder of the Hasidic movement in Jewish mysticism.

Fakhruddin Araqi   *See* Araqi.

Francis de Sales, St.   (1567–1622) French Catholic saint, revered for his practical teaching on the sanctification of daily life.

Francis of Assisi, St.   (c. 1181–1226) Probably the most universally loved of Catholic saints.

Gabirol, Solomon ibn   (c. 1021–c. 1058) Jewish poet, philosopher, and mystic in Muslim Spain.

gandharva   In Hinduism and Buddhism, a celestial being, comparable to angels in Abrahamic traditions.

Gandhi, M. K. (Mahatma)   (1869–1948) Indian spiritual and political leader known for *satyagraha,* his systematic method for resolving conflict through nonviolence.

Gita   *See* Bhagavad Gita.

Halevy, Judah   (c. 1075–1141) Jewish author and philosopher, often considered the greatest poet of the golden age of Hebrew poetry in Spain.

Hasan al-Basri   (642–728) Arab mystic revered for helping to lay the foundations of Islamic mysticism in the generation following the Prophet.

Hasan Kaimi Baba   (d. 1691) Sufi poet from Bosnia.

Inayat Khan, Hazrat   (1882–1927) Indian-born founder of the Sufi Order International.

Isaiah   Probably the most widely quoted book of the Jewish prophets, c. 6th century BC.

Isha Upanishad   Mahatma Gandhi's favorite of the Upanishads.

Jalaluddin Rumi   *See* Rumi, Jalaluddin.

kaaba   The holiest place in Islam, a shrine within the Sacred Mosque at Mecca.

Kabir   (1440–1518) One of the greatest mystic poets of India, claimed by both
   Sufi Muslims and Hindus and revered by Sikhs.

Katha Upanishad   The instructions of Yama, the king of death, to a sixteen-
   year-old seeker named Nachiketa.

Kook, Abraham Isaac, Rabbi   (1865–1935) A modern Jewish mystic.

Krishna   The Lord of Love, present in all; the Self within.

Lao Tzu   (c. 604–531 BC) Legendary Chinese sage whose collection of verses,
   the Tao Te Ching, is the basis of Taoism.

Lawrence, Brother   (b. Nicholas Herman, c. 1605–1691) Obscure lay brother
   in a Carmelite community in Paris, remembered for his letters on
   "practicing the presence of God" in everyday affairs.

maya   [Sanskrit] The illusion of separateness.

Mechtild of Magdeburg   (c. 1212–1282) A lay sister in a Catholic community
   in Germany, widely loved for her passionate devotional writing.

Meera   (c. 1498–1547) One of India's best-loved mystic poets, famous for her
   songs to Krishna.

Mishkat al-Masabih   A 14th-century collection of *hadith,* the sayings and
   actions of the Prophet Muhammad.

Nachiketa   Teenager in the Indian scriptures, particularly the Katha Upanishad,
   who goes to Yama, the king of death, to seek the meaning of life.

Nanak, Guru   (1469–1539) Punjabi saint, founder of the Sikh religion and
   revered by Hindus and Muslim Sufis.

nirvana   The Buddha's term for the extinction of all separateness.

Omkar, Swami   (1895–1982) Hindu mystic and teacher from South India.

Patrick, St.   (373?–493?) Christian saint, credited with bringing Christianity
   to Ireland.

Paul, St.   (b. ?–64? AD) Probably the most influential of the first-century
   Christian missionaries.

Psalms   Songs of worship traditionally composed by David, King of Israel
   (c. 1037–967 BC).

Qur'an   The central sacred text of Islam. "The Opening" (*Al-Fatiha*),
   the first verse of the Qur'an, is one of the essential affirmations of
   Islam, comparable to the Shema in Judaism and the Lord's Prayer in
   Christianity.

Rabi'a   (c. 717–801) A founding figure in the Sufi tradition of Islam.

Ramakrishna, Sri (1836–1886) A Hindu mystic. This selection is from a favorite song; its composer is unknown.

Ravidas (1399?–1518?) Hindu poet and mystic also revered by Sikhs and Sufis; brother-disciple of Kabir and perhaps a teacher to Meera.

Razi, Fakhraddin (1149–1209) Persian Muslim philosopher and scholar.

Rig Veda One of the Vedas, the four foundational scriptures of Hinduism.

Rumi, Jalaluddin (1207–1273) A Sufi master and one of the greatest of Persia's mystical poets.

Sarada Devi, Sri (1853–1920) Wife of Sri Ramakrishna, revered by his followers as Holy Mother.

Seng Ts'an (d. 606) Chinese sage, the Third Patriarch of Ch'an (Zen) Buddhism.

Shabestari, Mahmud (c. 1250–1320) Persian poet and mystic, contemporary with Araqi and Rumi.

Shantideva An 8th-century Indian Buddhist monk and mystic.

Shema The central affirmation of the Jewish faith.

Shvetashvatara Upanishad One of the most beautiful of the Upanishads, dedicated to God as Shiva.

Symeon the New Theologian, St. (949–1022) Greek Orthodox mystic and poet.

Teresa of Avila, St. (1515–1582) One of the best-loved of Catholic saints and mystics.

Thérèse of Lisieux, St. (1873–1897) Catholic saint and mystic who taught a "little way" of loving God in the midst of everyday affairs.

Thomas à Kempis (c. 1380–1471) Member of the Brethren of the Common Life, a lay monastic community in Holland; traditional author of *The Imitation of Christ,* the source of these selections.

Torah The five books of Moses (from Genesis to Deuteronomy) that begin the Jewish scriptures.

Tukaram (c. 1598–1650) Hindu mystic and devotional poet.

Upanishads The mystical documents of the Vedas, the center of India's scriptural canon.

Yama Personification of death in the Indian scriptures.

Yellow Lark, Chief Nineteenth-century Lakota elder.

Acknowledgments

Unless noted below, translations from Indian languages are by Eknath Easwaran. Otherwise, if no acknowledgment appears here, the translator is unknown.

Blue Mountain Center of Meditation: from *God Makes the Rivers to Flow,* comp. Eknath Easwaran (Nilgiri Press, 1982, 2003): Michael N. Nagler, "Entering into Joy" (p. 145); Stephen H. Ruppenthal, translations from Lao Tzu (pp. 37, 89, 130, 141), "Believing in Mind" (161), "The Miracle of Illumination" (p. 76), "The Island" (p. 193), "Discourse on Good Will" (p. 61); James Wehlage, translations of St. Teresa of Avila (pp. 40, 189, 204); Ellen Lehmann Beeler, "Shema" (p. 195); Rabbi Harvey Spivak, "Beloved of the Soul" (p. 59) & "Duties of the Heart" (p. 165)

Hoskins, Anthony (c. 1613): Translations of Thomas à Kempis (pp. 53, 92, 202) from *Of the Imitation of Christ* (Oxford, 1903)

Jewish Publication Society: Psalms 23, 24, 63, 100, 139 (pp. 60, 154, 148, 134, 124)

Nicholson, Reynold A.: "Only God I Saw" (p. 123), from R. A. Nicholson, *The Mystics of Islam* (G. Bell, 1914)

Paulist Press: "Radiant Is the World Soul" (p. 38), from *Abraham Isaac Kook,* tr. Ben Zion Bokser (Paulist Press, 1978)

Ramakrishna-Vivekananda Center of New York: "A Song from Ramakrishna" (p. 180), from *The Gospel of Sri Ramakrishna,* by "M.", tr. Swami Nikhilananda (© Swami Nikhilananda 1942); "The Whole World Is Your Own" (p. 84), from Swami Nikhilananda, *Holy Mother* (© Swami Nikhilananda 1962)

Ripley, G.: "A Sea of Peace" (p. 104), from *Life and Doctrine of Saint Catherine of Genoa* (n.p., 1874)

Singh, Sir Jogendra: "Invocations" (p. 63), from *The Persian Mystics: The Invocations of Sheikh Abdullah Ansari of Herat* (J. Murray, 1939)

Star, Jonathan: "The Shining Essence" (p. 152) & "The Mirror of This World" (p. 96) from *The Inner Treasure: An Introduction to the World's Sacred and Mystical Writings* (Tarcher / Putnam, © Jonathan Star 1999); "A Garden Beyond Paradise" (p. 149) from *A Garden beyond Paradise: The Mystical Poetry of Rumi*, ed. Jonathan Star & Shahram Shiva (© Jonathan Star, Bantam, 1992); Psalm 119 ("I Am the One Who Will Never Forget You," p. 77) from *Two Suns Rising: A Collection of Sacred Writings* (Bantam, 1991; © Jonathan Star 1991)

Sufi Order International: "Prayer for the Peace of the World" (p. 136) & "Prayer for Peace" (p. 147)

Tagore, Rabindranath: "The Unstruck Bells and Drums" (p. 51), from *Songs of Kabir* (Macmillan, 1915)

Vedanta Society of Southern California: "United in Heart" (p. 135), from *Prayers and Meditations Compiled from the Scriptures of India*, ed. Swami Prabhavananda & Clive Johnson (Vedanta Press, 1967)

Washington Province of Discalced Carmelites: "Living on Love" (p. 138) from *The Poetry of St. Thérèse of Lisieux*, tr. Donald Kinney, OCD. © Washington Province of Discalced Carmelites 1995 (Washington, DC: ICS Publications, 1995)

Index by Author & Source

Index by Title & First Line

THE BLUE MOUNTAIN CENTER OF MEDITATION

The Blue Mountain Center of Meditation publishes Easwaran's books, videos, and audios, and offers retreats on his eight-point program of passage meditation. For more information:

The Blue Mountain Center of Meditation
Box 256, Tomales, California 94971
Telephone: +1 707 878 2369
Toll-free in the US: 800 475 2369
Facsimile: +1 707 878 2375
E-mail: info@easwaran.org
www.easwaran.org

NILGIRI PRESS

"This is the secret of meditation: we become what we meditate on."

– Eknath Easwaran

This companion volume to *Timeless Wisdom* is an introduction to Easwaran's method of meditation, in which we choose inspirational passages that embody our highest ideals and send them deep into consciousness through slow, sustained attention. Our passages become lifelines, taking us to the source of wisdom deep within and then guiding us through the challenges of daily life.

Universal and dogma-free, passage meditation is part of Easwaran's eight-point program of practical skills. Based on traditional spiritual practices but adjusted for modern lifestyles, *Passage Meditation* goes step by step through each point of Easwaran's program, showing us how to stay calm and focused at work and at home.

NILGIRI PRESS

THE BOOKS OF EKNATH EASWARAN

CLASSICS OF INDIAN SPIRITUALITY

These timeless, universal texts from the Indian wisdom traditions address the fundamental questions of life. Speaking to us directly, all three classics assure us if we make wise choices, everything that matters in life is within human reach. All three editions by Easwaran are best-sellers in their class.

"No one in modern times is more qualified – no, make that 'as qualified' – to translate the epochal Classics of Indian Spirituality than Eknath Easwaran. And the reason is clear. It is impossible to get to the heart of those classics unless you live them, and he did live them. My admiration of the man and his works is boundless."

– Huston Smith,
author of *The World's Religions*

NILGIRI PRESS

THE BOOKS OF EKNATH EASWARAN

CLASSICS OF INDIAN SPIRITUALITY

BHAGAVAD GITA

Prince Arjuna, despairing on the battlefield of life, receives profound teachings from his spiritual guide, Sri Krishna, on life, work, love, and the immortal Self.

DHAMMAPADA

This collection of the Buddha's teachings is permeated with all the power and practicality of one of the world's most appealing spiritual guides.

UPANISHADS

In these most ancient of Indian wisdom texts, illumined sages share flashes of insight, the result of many years of investigation into consciousness itself.

NILGIRI PRESS

Publisher's Cataloging-In-Publication Data

(Prepared by The Donohue Group, Inc.)

Easwaran, Eknath.

  Timeless wisdom : passages for meditation from the world's saints & sages / Eknath Easwaran. -- 1st ed.

  p. ; cm.

  "This book is a compact edition of a fuller anthology, God makes the rivers to flow, with a new preface and additional passages."

  ISBN: 978-1-58638-027-4

1. Meditations. 2. Religious literature. I. Title. II. Title: God makes the rivers to flow.

BL624.2 .E172 2008

204.32   2008921640